UNDERSTANDING
DAVID HENRY HWANG

UNDERSTANDING CONTEMPORARY AMERICAN LITERATURE
Matthew J. Bruccoli, Founding Editor
Linda Wagner-Martin, Series Editor

Volumes on

Edward Albee | Sherman Alexie | Nelson Algren | Paul Auster
Nicholson Baker | John Barth | Donald Barthelme | The Beats
Thomas Berger | The Black Mountain Poets | Robert Bly | T. C. Boyle
Raymond Carver | Fred Chappell | Chicano Literature
Contemporary American Drama | Contemporary American Horror Fiction
Contemporary American Literary Theory
Contemporary American Science Fiction, 1926–1970
Contemporary American Science Fiction, 1970–2000
Contemporary Chicana Literature | Robert Coover | Philip K. Dick
James Dickey | E. L. Doctorow | Rita Dove | John Gardner | George Garrett
Tim Gautreaux | John Hawkes | Joseph Heller | Lillian Hellman | Beth Henley
James Leo Herlihy | David Henry Hwang | John Irving | Randall Jarrell
Charles Johnson | Diane Johnson | Adrienne Kennedy | William Kennedy
Jack Kerouac | Jamaica Kincaid | Etheridge Knight | Tony Kushner
Ursula K. Le Guin | Denise Levertov | Bernard Malamud | David Mamet
Bobbie Ann Mason | Colum McCann | Cormac McCarthy | Jill McCorkle
Carson McCullers | W. S. Merwin | Arthur Miller | Lorrie Moore
Toni Morrison's Fiction | Vladimir Nabokov | Gloria Naylor | Joyce Carol Oates
Tim O'Brien | Flannery O'Connor | Cynthia Ozick | Suzan-Lori Parks
Walker Percy | Katherine Anne Porter | Richard Powers | Reynolds Price
Annie Proulx | Thomas Pynchon | Theodore Roethke | Philip Roth | May Sarton
Hubert Selby, Jr. | Mary Lee Settle | Sam Shepard | Neil Simon
Isaac Bashevis Singer | Jane Smiley | Gary Snyder | William Stafford
Robert Stone | Anne Tyler | Gerald Vizenor | Kurt Vonnegut
David Foster Wallace | Robert Penn Warren | James Welch | Eudora Welty
Edmund White | Tennessee Williams | August Wilson | Charles Wright

UNDERSTANDING

DAVID HENRY HWANG

William C. Boles

The University of South Carolina Press

© 2013 University of South Carolina

Published by the University of South Carolina Press
Columbia, South Carolina 29208

www.sc.edu/uscpress

Manufactured in the United States of America

22 21 20 19 18 17 16 15 14 13   10 9 8 7 6 5 4 3 2 1

Library of Congress Cataloging-in-Publication Data

Boles, William C., 1966–
  Understanding David Henry Hwang / William C. Boles.
      pages cm. — (Understanding Contemporary American Literature)
  Includes bibliographical references and index.
    ISBN 978-1-61117-287-4 (hardbound : alk. paper) —
  ISBN 978-1-61117-288-1 (ebook) 1. Hwang, David Henry, 1957–
  —Criticism and interpretation. 1. Title.
    PS3558.W83Z55 2013
    812'.54—dc23

                                              2013013544

For my dad, J. W. "Bill" Boles
(1935–2013)

CONTENTS

SERIES EDITOR'S PREFACE

The Understanding Contemporary American Literature series was founded by the estimable Matthew J. Bruccoli (1931–2008), who envisioned these volumes as guides or companions for students as well as good nonacademic readers, a legacy that will continue as new volumes are developed to fill in gaps among the nearly one hundred series volumes published to date and to embrace a host of new writers only now making their marks on our literature.

As Professor Bruccoli explained in his preface to the volumes he edited, because much influential contemporary literature makes special demands, "the word understanding in the titles was chosen deliberately. Many willing readers lack an adequate understanding of how contemporary literature works; that is, of what the author is attempting to express and the means by which it is conveyed." Aimed at fostering this understanding of good literature and good writers, the criticism and analysis in the series provide instruction in how to read certain contemporary writers—explicating their material, language, structures, themes, and perspectives—and facilitate a more profitable experience of the works under discussion.

In the twenty-first century Professor Bruccoli's prescience gives us an avenue to publish expert critiques of significant contemporary American writing. The series continues to map the literary landscape and to provide both instruction and enjoyment. Future volumes will seek to introduce new voices alongside canonized favorites, to chronicle the changing literature of our times, and to remain, as Professor Bruccoli conceived, contemporary in the best sense of the word.

Linda Wagner-Martin, Series Editor

CHAPTER 1

Understanding David Henry Hwang

Sitting across from me in my American Drama class was David Henry Hwang. Surrounding us were students who had studied his play M. *Butterfly* the previous two class sessions and were ready to hear the real meaning of the play from the author instead of the interpretations of their teacher and fellow classmates. Hwang, though, like his play, surprised the students by asking each one to tell him what he or she found problematic in his Tony-Award–winning work. In other words, he wanted college students to tell him, a playwright for more than thirty years, what was wrong with his work, and in doing so he changed the discourse of the classroom from students listening to an expert to critics sharing their thoughts with a writer. In one subtle move he informed the students that their opinions and voices mattered to him. His opening question triggered a conversation that covered a wide range of topics, including whether the play was a love story, how each one of us inhabits multiple faces throughout our lives, and the changing nature of East/West relations, all with M. *Butterfly* as a background, but, equally, each student's life and experiences also became part of the discussion. After Hwang's visit to our class one student confided in me that it was one the most incredible experiences he had had in college.

The same level of excitement existed for all the students with whom he came in touch when he visited Rollins College in February 2010, as he led workshop sessions with new playwriting students, examining their work with a professionally keen eye as well as with great compassion; conducted a writing workshop with a group of students; and amiably made himself available to students with questions, comments, and advice. In the latter case his visit was an epiphany for an Asian American student, who shyly asked me if she could just have ten minutes to talk to Hwang, to which he gladly agreed. I later came to learn that she, like Hwang, was born to immigrant parents from Asia and wanted to write about her experience of bridging the American way of life with her parents' protective Cambodian perspective. The words of encouragement and advice he gave her provided her with the confidence to write a full-length screenplay about a first-generation girl with strict Cambodian parents. Her story is just one of many that came up during his three-day visit to our campus. As for me, watching his amiable interaction with our students, coteaching the playwriting workshop with him, chatting about the casting difficulties for his new play, *Chinglish,* and discussing the merits of the varying flavors of crunchy Cheetos inspired me to write this book so that I could understand more about the playwright who had such a profound experience on my students as well as on contemporary American drama.

David Henry Hwang is a first-generation Chinese American, having been born in California on August 11, 1957, to his two immigrant parents. His father, Henry Hwang, the second son of his family, was born to a Chinese peasant who had relocated from the Chinese countryside to Shanghai, where he became wealthy and where Henry was born. Feeling confined by the limitations placed upon him as the family's second son, Henry immigrated to Oregon in the late 1940s in order to study business at Linfield College before eventually transferring to the University of Southern California. His decision to leave China should not have come as a surprise to his family and friends. According to Hwang, his father "never much liked China, or the whole idea behind China or Chinese ways of thinking. He's always been much more attracted to American ways of thinking. He feels Americans are more open—they tell you what they think—and he's very much that way himself."[1] Henry's attraction to America in part grew out of the American movies he watched growing up. Hwang would incorporate his father's love of classic American movies and its stars to comedic as well as dramatic effect in *Yellow Face.*

His mother, Dorothy Huang, also had a Chinese background. Her grandparents had lived in Amoy but moved to the Philippines, where they became successful merchants. Her family members were devout Protestant fundamentalists, and the religious faith of his mother's side of the family would significantly influence his two plays *Family Devotions* and *Golden Child.* Following in the footsteps of her brother, who had come to the United States to go to college, Dorothy immigrated in 1952 in order to study concert piano at the University of Southern California. Dorothy met Henry at a university dance, and they hit it off. In order for Dorothy to accept Henry's proposal of marriage, he had to convert to Christianity, which he willingly did. Henry and Dorothy seamlessly assimilated into American culture, so much so that their three children grew up with a fairly stereotypical American childhood, rather than navigating the intricacies of a mixed cultural experience. Hwang admitted that his parents' assimilation was a crucial component of his personal and artistic progress. He explained, "My whole personal political development is largely a reaction to the fact that my parents did assimilate. If they had been more traditional and tied to the root culture, I would probably be a completely different person."[2]

David Henry Hwang is the eldest child and only son of Henry and Dorothy, who also had two younger daughters, Mimi and Grace. The three Hwang siblings were raised in the comfortable enclave of San Gabriel, California, in the San Gabriel Valley. Hwang has admitted that he never really attributed any significance to being Chinese because he and his sisters were not raised with that mindset. "We were raised pretty much as white European Americans in terms of the things we celebrated. There's an odd confluence in my family between a father who decided to turn away from things Chinese and a mother whose family had been converted to Christianity in China several generations back. Consequently between the two of them there was no particular desire for us to speak Chinese or celebrate Chinese holidays at all."[3] For a short period of time, the Hwangs did enroll their children in a Chinese-language course, but, shortly thereafter, they pulled them out, fearing that if they learned Chinese their English studies would be disrupted. While Hwang knew that he was of Chinese heritage, "it never occurred to me that that had any particular implication or that it should differentiate me in any way. I thought it was a minor detail, like having red hair. I never got a lot in school to contradict that. My parents brought us up with a rather nice sense of self."[4]

And yet, while in some interviews Hwang described his childhood as a Chinese American in the 1960s and 1970s as fairly idyllic and painless in terms of racial issues (he noted at one point that he never experienced any racism until he first went to New York City), at other times he admitted being aware of racial stereotypes and bigotry tied to popular perceptions of Asians and Asian Americans, especially when Hollywood was involved. He experienced "a certain discomfort while watching Asian characters portrayed in film and television. Whether it was 'the enemy' in Japanese, Korean, or Vietnam War movies or the obsequious figure—*Bonanza*'s cook, Hop Sing, for instance—all of these people made me feel embarrassed, frankly. You could argue that that was the beginning of some impulse that led me to create my own Asian characters later in life."[5] His discomfort with these broad and, at times, nefarious depictions had an effect on his interaction with these stereotypes, as "I would go out of my way not to watch movies or television shows featuring Asian characters. If asked to explain, I might simply have replied that they made me feel 'icky.' They were consistently inhuman: either inhumanly bad (Fu Manchu, Japanese soldiers) or inhumanly good (Charlie Chan, Asian ingenues who died for the love of a white B-movie actor)."[6] This contradiction between his own experiences as an Asian American and those of characters on his television screen would prove to be driving fodder for most of his plays as he constantly questions the nature of identity (whether it be ethnic, familial, religious, national, or societal) through the use or disruption of stereotypes, while also exploring the challenging question of what makes someone authentically ethnic. "As a playwright, I find that much of my work has involved a search for authenticity; if I could discover more truthful images to replace the stereotypical ones of my youth, perhaps I could also begin to understand my own identity. As part of this exploration, I have often taken older stories and reinvented them on my own terms."[7] And, in having such a pursuit throughout his career, "I have become less interested in seeking some holy grail of authenticity and more convinced of the need to create characters who burst from the page or stage with the richness, complexity and contradictions of real people."[8]

While he lived in an assimilated household and was engaged in a typical American childhood, he still maintained connections to his Chinese heritage through stories shared with him by his parents and his grandparents. When he was ten, he learned that his maternal grandmother was sick. "I remember thinking that if anything happened to her, our family's history would be lost forever."[9] In order to prevent such an occurrence, he received permission from his parents to travel to the Philippines to see her. While there, he recorded his grandmother's stories about their family and transcribed them into a ninety-page history of his mother's side of the family. "I distributed it to the family and it was well received. I suppose that was the first real writing I did."[10] This piece of juvenilia would later become the basis for Hwang's second Broadway play, *Golden Child,* which dramatized his mother's family's conversion to Christianity as well as the aftershocks of their embracing Western religion. Because of their mother's faith, the Hwang children were raised with a fundamentalist background, which included attending church during much of the weekend (at a fundamentalist church that had been founded by his great-uncle), Bible study in the middle of the week, and prayers at every meal. He described their worship as a "weird Chinese American Baptist evangelical fusion."[11]

As the children grew up, Hwang's mother taught piano at Azusa Pacific College and at the Colburn School of the Arts, while also performing professionally in the Los Angeles area. His mother's piano playing was what introduced Hwang to the theater for the first time. When he was eight years old, his mother played the piano for a production of Gian Carlo Menotti's *The Medium* at East West Players, and Hwang accompanied her to rehearsals. While his mother taught and played piano, his father was a successful accountant. In the early 1970s Henry had his opportunity to achieve not only greater financial success but also the American Dream by becoming one of the founders of the Far East National Bank, the first federally chartered Asian American bank in the continental United States. In a bizarre twist, which Hwang would use as a comedic centerpiece of *Family Devotions,* shortly after the bank opened, his father was kidnapped and held for a three-hundred-thousand-dollar ransom. His abductors drove him around Los Angeles until the money was paid. Once the kidnappers received the ransom, he was released. The police never apprehended the culprits.

During elementary school, Hwang took up the violin, which he still plays today. Like his mother with her piano playing, Hwang's skill at the violin connected him to the theatre. As a high school student, he played in the orchestra for various musical productions. About these early experiences in the theater, Hwang remarked, "The only thing that was strange was that I liked to stay after rehearsal and listen to the director give notes."[12] In college he switched from classical violin, which he found boring, to jazz violin. In addition to his musical skills, Hwang was also a champion debater in high school. He first attended San Gabriel High School and then, because of his debating prowess, was recruited by Harvard School, to which he transferred. Hwang has credited both these activities with being beneficial to his later career as a playwright: "Music really helps in terms of developing structure and dramatic growth, and jazz in particular helps with theatrical improvisation. As a jazz musician you get used to peaks and valleys and tensions—and these same things occur in theater which, like music, is a time art. And my early interest in debate no doubt contributed to my theatrical interest in the opposition of ideas and the interplay of ideas in many plays."[13] However, because of his musical background, he approaches playwriting with a slightly different perspective than that of many of his contemporaries. "I still don't pay that much attention to particular words, just like you don't pay attention to the individual notes on a score: It's about the movement that they create."[14]

After graduating from high school, Hwang attended Stanford University, assuming that after graduation he would enroll in law school. Expecting him to follow in the path of his father, his parents wanted him to earn a business degree, which would have been difficult since Stanford did not offer a degree in business. By the time he graduated, though, he knew he would not be pursuing either profession. While at Stanford, Hwang had three epiphanies, all of which would prove instrumental to his writing career. The first epiphany occurred when, in his sophomore year, he began to question his religious upbringing and eventually threw off his family's Christian beliefs: "I have to say that breaking away was one of the things I'm most proud of in my life. It really was something I had to do to get my muscles to work for me. But because my family was monolithically Christian, I thought it would separate me from my family forever," which did not happen.[15] Despite his personal choice to leave the church, religion played an important element in three of his plays. In addition to *Golden Child,* with its focus on his own family's religious conversion, *Family Devotions* focuses on the visit of a relative from China who has a profound effect on not only the religious identities of the family members but also the entire religious basis of the family's history, while *Rich Relations* explores the concept of resurrection, as one character comes back to life after being dead for an hour and another character attempts to restart his identity.

The second epiphany revolved around his ethnicity. As a student, he began to seek answers to that awkwardness he had felt as a child when watching depictions of Asian characters on television. He immersed himself in an exploration of Asian and Asian American issues. He lived in an all-Asian residence hall; played the electric violin, which he took up in college, as a member of an all-Asian rock band called Bamboo, whose sole existence was to play "Asian-American protest music";[16] "became involved with these Asian, Marxist oriented, consciousness-raising groups";[17] and studied works by Asian American writers. In the process of this submersion in all things Asian, he became a professed "isolationist nationalist."[18] One of the most influential works he read was Maxine Hong Kingston's *The Woman Warrior.* Kingston's work "made me feel that I could find my own voice. As an Asian-American, she was the first author who spoke in a voice that seemed special, directly related to *me.* Before reading her work, I didn't think it was possible to write about my own parochial concerns; they didn't seem to have a place in literature as such."[19] The consciousness raising would have long-term reverberations through his work, as he would explore in all of his plays the juxtapositions and tensions between the East and the West, including issues of identity, as in *FOB* and *The Dance and the Railroad;* Western male conceptions about Eastern women, explored in *M. Butterfly* and *Flower Drum Song;* the tension between the temptations of Western modernity and the traditional notions of the East, as presented in *Family Devotions* and *Golden Child;* and the rising economic superpower status of China contrasted to the struggling position of the United States, as shown in *Chinglish.*

The third and most important collegiate epiphany concerned his eventual career. At Harvard, his high school, he had seen Arthur Kopits's *Indians;* then, as a first-year student at Stanford, he visited the American Conservatory Theatre, attending performances of William Shakespeare's *A Winter's Tale* and Thornton Wilder's *The Matchmaker.* He found that "creating a world and then seeing it come to life seemed very appealing."[20] So, in his sophomore year, he decided he wanted to become a playwright. He submitted a draft of a play to John L'Heureux, a creative-writing teacher at Stanford and also a novelist, who told the fledgling playwright that his writing was problematic because his draft indicated that he had no comprehension of the distinct structure of a play. L'Heureux recommended that, before writing any more plays, Hwang read representative works from the genre. Hwang immediately began reading plays by contemporary playwrights, many of whom became influences on his later plays. One of the first plays he read was *Tooth of Crime* by Sam Shepard, who would become a major influence on his early work. Ntozake Shange's *for colored girls who have considered suicide when the rainbow is enuf* was also eye-opening because of its "freeform theatricality"; for the actors, "nothing physically on stage [is] holding them back."[21] Other plays and playwrights that ended up influencing him as a student and later in his career as a playwright include Harold Pinter's *The Birthday Party,* Tom Stoppard's *Rosencrantz and Guildenstern Are Dead,* Shepard's *Buried Child,* Peter Shaffer's *Amadeus,* and David Mamet's *Glengarry Glen Ross.*

In the summer of 1978, between his junior and senior years, he participated in a summer internship at Padua Hills Playwrights Festival, which included the opportunity to work directly with Sam Shepard, who would win the Pulitzer Prize for *Buried Child* the next year, and Maria Irene Fornes, author of *Fefu and Her Friends* and *MUD.* During a writing exercise, directed by Fornes, the germ of an idea formed. "I just found that this stuff appeared on the page, this stuff about East-West issues, about China, about immigration, assimilation, all this kind of stuff."[22] This mixture of topics would become his first play, *FOB,* which stands for "fresh off the boat," and Hwang directed its first production in his residence hall as part of his senior project. In 1979 Hwang graduated from Stanford with a distinction in English, a membership in Phi Beta Kappa, and, because of the strength of *FOB,* his parents' blessing to pursue playwriting.

Hwang sent the play off to the Eugene O'Neill Theater Center, where it was accepted for its workshop. After the O'Neill production, the powerful and influential New York City producer Joseph Papp picked up the play's option, producing it off-Broadway at his Public Theater in June 1980. After the

O'Neill workshop and before the premiere of his play in New York, Hwang returned to California and taught English for a year at Menlo-Atherton High School near San Francisco before returning east in the fall of 1980 to enroll in Yale's School of Drama. Hwang attended Yale for the 1980–1981 academic year and completed all the required course work, continuing his education in the history of theater. He left in the spring of 1981 because the subsequent two years of the program were workshop intensive. Since *FOB* had already been produced off-Broadway before he even matriculated and because, while he was at Yale, his second play *The Dance and the Railroad,* about a strike by Chinese workers on the transcontinental railroad, had premiered off-off Broadway before moving to the Public and a third play, *Family Devotions,* was to debut in the fall of 1981 at the Public, he felt that spending two years workshopping plays would be superfluous. With his departure from Yale, he moved from being a full-time student to working as a full-time writer. Two years later, in 1983, *Sound and Beauty,* composed of two one-act plays, *The Sound of a Voice* and *The House of the Sleeping Beauties,* which were inspired by Japanese literature and films, premiered at the Public Theater.

As he wrote these early works, he developed a three-step process, which he still uses, for writing his plays. Hwang's plays always stem from a question that he wants to answer. Perhaps the most representative example of a prompting question occurred before he started writing *M. Butterfly.* Upon hearing about a twenty-year affair during which a French diplomat never knew that his Chinese lover was another man, Hwang asked how the French man could not have known. How could he have unknowingly engaged in an affair with someone of the same sex for so long? It was the urge to find the answer to this question that prompted him to write *M. Butterfly.* Once Hwang finds his question, he then decides how his story will begin and end. However, how he gets from the beginning to the end is completely open to the whim of his subconscious mind and his creativity. Hwang has likened this part of his writing process to a cross-country journey. For example, suppose your starting point is New York City and your end point is Los Angeles. There are infinite paths that will get you from one point to the other, and that journey is what his writing process and, eventually, the entire play is about. *Chinglish* perfectly exemplifies this method. He knew that the beginning would feature an American businessman who goes to China to close a business deal, and "I knew that the end would find the man successful, but for all the wrong reasons."[23] He then had to write the story between these two points. The final step is that he always looks to other playwrights to help provide a framework for the structure of his plays. Hwang admitted: "I've been a pretty blatant thief in modeling various plays on work by other playwrights."[24] When he wrote *Golden Child*, he looked back to Anton Chekhov and *The Three Sisters* because he wanted to capture a similar sense of the smaller moments of domestic life that Chekhov conveyed so well. In looking to past and present writers, he uses their narrative structures to help inspire his play's framework, enabling him to answer the pressing question driving the work and also helping him craft the journey between the opening and the closing points of his story.

Hwang's ascension over four years from anonymous college student to Public Theater mainstay (with four productions at Papp's Public Theater) was unprecedented for an Asian American voice. With his meteoric rise he suddenly found himself defined as *the* Asian American writer for theater. With this moniker attached to him, he experienced intense pressure and creative uncertainty because he and his work were being identified only through his ethnic identity. He admitted to a great deal of confusion at this point of his career: "I didn't see the point in what I was doing."[25] He went from being a productive playwright with an average of one produced play a year between 1980 and 1983 to a struggling writer who would take three years to write his next play. During the period of nonwriting, he traveled around the world, and in Toronto, Canada, he met Ophelia Y. M. Chong, a Chinese Canadian artist. They married in 1985. His marriage to Ophelia stabilized his writing, and his next play, *Rich Relations,* was produced in 1986. However, the play distinctly shifted from his earlier Asian and Asian American works, as he deliberately pushed back against the Asian-artist identity by writing a play that featured only Caucasian characters. For numerous reasons, *Rich Relations* failed. Surprisingly, the failure turned out to be a groundbreaking moment for Hwang, who found his failure to be incredibly liberating, erasing the previous expectations that had been heaped upon him. He suddenly found that he could turn to his writing without the pressure he had been experiencing. With this newfound freedom, Hwang wrote the most successful play of his career, the international smash *M. Butterfly*, which has been produced in more than forty countries. *M. Butterfly* won Hwang a Tony for best play, and a Hollywood studio adapted the play into a film, which featured Hwang's screenplay adaptation. Shortly after his success with *M. Butterfly,* his marriage to Ophelia sputtered, and they divorced in 1989. A few years later, in December of 1993, Hwang married Kathryn Layng, a theater and television actress, who performed in the Broadway production of *M. Butterfly* and was a regular on the television show *Doogie Howser, M.D.*, which is now best remembered for starring a young Neil Patrick Harris. Hwang and Layng later became parents to two children, Noah and Eva.

While Hwang's earlier successes had garnered him attention as a success-ful Asian American voice, it was the strength of *M. Butterfly* that catapulted him to national and international status, especially because he was the first and still the only Asian American to have his plays produced on Broadway. In accomplishing such a groundbreaking feat for Asian Americans, Hwang received deserved recognition and praise, but he also became a target of criti-cism, especially among the Asian American community. After all, when only one voice of an entire ethnic group is recognized by the establishment, as it was in Hwang's case in the theatrical community, then the various factions in that ethnic group want to ensure that their perspectives are being expressed by the newly chosen representative. It is not surprising that Hwang found himself in a no-win situation when it came to pleasing the entirety of the Asian American community. Some openly questioned his credentials to be a representative voice because of his affluent background and his comfortable childhood free of racial strife. In addition to the questions about Hwang's personal background were more specific queries when it came to the politics of the Asian community, as he was a target from both the left and the right: "The right tends to feel the dirty laundry issues, whereas for the left the fact that I've been relatively successful in a mainstream market has always made me somewhat politically suspect. I've 'whited-out' too much, as it were."[26] Like any good debater, Hwang understands the reason for the criticism and can sympathize with both sides of the argument. "This is a community that is generally not represented well at all on the stage, in the media, etc. So on those few occasions when something comes along, everybody feels obligated to make sure that it represents his own point of view. And of course no artist can do that."[27] And yet, despite his ability to rationalize the criticism he has received, he still acknowledges the difficulty of hearing "that you've set the Asian-American back 10 years."[28]

Hwang has been adamant about his initial desire to be a writer and noth-ing more than a writer. "I didn't set out to be a political spokesperson or a figure representing an ethnic group. I set out wanting to be a playwright. All this other stuff has come about as a consequence, I suppose, of whatever success I've been able to have as a writer."[29] One of his most vocal critics has been Frank Chin, whose works from the 1970s were important influences in Hwang's own writing and exploration of ethnic identity. Chin called Hwang, as well as Amy Tan and Maxine Hong Kingston, a fake Asian in his essay "Come All Ye Asian American Writers of the Real and the Fake." When asked about Chin, Hwang dismissed the criticism as growing out of jealousy on Chin's part because Chin came before them and missed out on the recog-nition that current Asian American writers were receiving. "When evaluating works of art, I believe some critics misrepresent the community by speaking or writing as if it were a unified monolith. When such critics say a particular artist's work does or does not accurately portray the community, they are actually evaluating whether the work reflects the *critic's* vision of the community. By ignoring this fact, they attempt to deny their own subjectivity."[30] Hwang also found that his rise to prominence was problematic for Asian American scholars, such as Esther Lee Kim.[31] She asked, "Is he the 'token' Asian American in mainstream theatre? How else do we explain the fact that he continues to be the only Asian American playwright to be produced on Broadway?"[32] Throughout his career Hwang would continue to face similar questions about and criticism of his role as one of the most widely recognized and representative voices of Asian Americans.

During the 1980s Hwang had six plays produced off or on Broadway. That decade would prove to be his most prolific in terms of his playwriting, as the ensuing decades would not see the same number of full-length plays being produced. No doubt part of the reason for the reduction in his productivity stemmed from writing opportunities that appeared after the success of *M. Butterfly*. Hollywood came calling, and he wrote numerous screenplays (some produced, some not), in addition to adapting his own *M. Butterfly*. In addition, The Walt Disney Company hired him to work on the book for two of its Broadway musicals, *Aida* and *Tarzan*. Most of his productivity, though, has come in the realm of opera, as he has become the most produced contemporary American librettist, including four collaborations with Philip Glass.

Hwang's raised level of celebrity drew him into a major controversy in 1990 surrounding the Broadway transfer of the London smash hit musical *Miss Saigon*, starring Jonathan Pryce as a Eurasian pimp, a role he originated in the West End. Hwang and other Asian Americans protested the casting, calling it a blatant example of "yellowface," that is, the casting of a non-Asian actor as an Asian character. Despite the fiery protest and the media storm of coverage about the controversy, the musical eventually opened on Broadway with Pryce in the role as the Engineer. Hwang's next two plays would, in turn, set out to explore and explode stereotypes surrounding a variety of ethnicities. The first was produced in 1992 and was a one-act piece called *Bondage,* which was set in an S&M parlor with a man and a woman in full gear, including masks, playing out various interracial pairings. The piece was a personal play for Hwang because the conversations about race between Layng, who is Caucasian, and the playwright influenced the role playing of his characters. A much more directed response to *Miss Saigon* was a farce called *Face Value,* about an actor in yellowface whose casting causes major chaos on opening night. The comedy turned out to be Hwang's biggest failure, as it closed on Broadway in previews in 1993. However, as with *Rich Relations,* the failure of *Face Value* was not devastating but liberating, as it removed the onus of having to write a play that outshone his masterpiece, *M. Butterfly.* It would not be until 1998, ten years after *M. Butterfly*'s premiere, that he would finally return to opening a play on Broadway with *Golden Child.*

After his success with *Aida* for Disney in 2000, Hwang undertook a significant musical project, deciding to rewrite the book to Richard Rodgers and Oscar Hammerstein's *Flower Drum Song,* which had been a successful musical adaptation in the late 1950s of C. Y. Lee's book of the same name. Hwang worked closely with the Rodgers and Hammerstein estate, rewriting the book for a more contemporary audience. It premiered on Broadway in 2002 but was not a commercial success. While he would write a number of ten-minute plays for various compilation evenings, ten years would pass between the 1998 production of *Golden Child* and Hwang's next full-length dramatic work, *Yellow Face,* which was both a far more successful comedic return to the *Miss Saigon* controversy about authentic ethnic identity and an attack on various governmental and institutional racial biases against Asians, particularly Chinese, that were prevalent in the 1990s. Its success re-energized Hwang, who decided to rededicate himself to playwriting. Hwang's third Broadway play, *Chinglish,* was produced in 2011. In order to be true to the Chinese characters in the play, who outnumber the Western ones, Hwang wrote a quarter of the play in Mandarin Chinese and relied on supertitles and translators (some of whom provide comedic moments) for the non-Mandarin-speaking Western audience. In the 2012–2013 season, Hwang was the featured playwright at the Signature Theatre off-Broadway in New York. During the theatrical season 2012–2013, the company revived *The Dance and the Railroad* and *Golden Child,* and at the start of the 2013–2014 season it will produce the world premiere of his latest play *Kung Fu,* about Bruce Lee. Over the past few years, Hwang has made it clear that his career as a playwright has found its second wind, which, while it is good for Hwang, is even better for his audience and the American theater.

CHAPTER 2

Hwang's Asian American Trilogy
FOB, *The Dance and the Railroad,*
and *Family Devotions*

FOB

The inspiration for *FOB,* Hwang's first play, occurred when Hwang attended the Padua Hills Playwrights Festival between his junior and senior years at Stanford University. The summer experience proved to be a catalyst for his playwriting, highlighted by his work with Maria Irene Fornes. One of her writing exercises, which Hwang still uses in writing workshops with students, fueled the creation of *FOB.* For twenty minutes the participants wrote a scene. She then restarted the creative process but with the new requirement that the writers had to incorporate into their writing a word or phrase that she would randomly call out. Hwang remarked on the exercise's effectiveness in unlocking the writer's subconscious and emotional interests: "I've always been comfortable with my intellectual side and skittish with my emotional side. Emotional repression is part of my legacy as Chinese. And Irene's insistence on unlocking that and on giving a lot of freedom irrespective of formal structures was extremely useful to me."[1] During this writing drill, his questions about ethnicity and his own Chinese American identity began to appear, leading to the main issues at *FOB*'s core. The draft he began that summer with Fornes developed into the full-length play that he directed on March 2, 1979, at his Asian American residence hall, the Junipero House, during his senior year at Stanford.

One of the most influential critics of Hwang's chosen vocation as a playwright was his father, who wanted his son to emulate him and become a businessman. Needless to say, he was not enthusiastic about his son's artistic inclination. Both Hwangs tell different versions of what occurred when the son shared a draft of *FOB* with his father. According to David, Henry saw profanity in the text and turned to his son, remarking, "I sent you to Stanford and you write this junk?"[2] In Henry's version, he agreed that he refused to finish reading the play. However, his rationale for rejecting the script was different: "I was an illiterate. I'd never read an English book from beginning to end. To me, writing plays was not serious. It was not for lawyers or doctors. It was a pastime. And I said to my wife, 'I send him to an expensive school and all he is doing is writing these plays?'"[3] However, both agreed that when his father learned that *FOB* was going to be directed by his son and produced at Stanford, Henry told Dorothy, "Well, you know we have to see this and we'll decide whether this is good or bad, and if it's bad we have to discourage him from doing this."[4] Despite Henry's initial inclination to dissuade David from his artistic pursuits, when he saw the play performed he found himself emotionally overcome. In remembering the evening, he said: "I didn't have a clue what I was going to see, but for the first time in my life, I was so touched, so moved, that I was crying like a baby. It was about our lives, about how we came over. It was so moving. An incredible experience. It's something I'll remember the rest of my life."[5] After the performance ended, Henry decided to support his son's choice to be a playwright.

Encouraged by his teachers and friends, Hwang sent *FOB* to the Eugene O'Neill National Playwrights Conference, where it was one of only twelve plays to be selected for workshop and development in July 1979. After the O'Neill, Hwang and *FOB* came to the attention of producer Joseph Papp, who decided to produce the play at the Public Theater. The play had its Manhattan premiere on June 8, 1980. Papp related to the play because the characters' experiences recalled his own familiarity with the lives of Eastern European Jewish immigrants: "Even though the cultures were strikingly different, it was the same notion. The principle of someone coming from the old country who didn't know how to behave himself was very much part of my own tradition."[6] However, Papp also appreciated the complexity of the work. He explained: "*FOB* went into the traditions by suddenly moving into a more abstract, poetic existence in the context of a very naturalistic play."[7] Papp's support of Hwang's work would prove instrumental in the young playwright's rapid ascent into the New York City theatrical world, as Papp would be the producer of Hwang's first four works, all of which appeared at the Public. In a mere two years Hwang's first play developed from the inkling of an idea produced by a subconscious awakening workshop with Fornes to a heralded off-Broadway production.[8]

While the larger thematic concept of Chinese American identity was generated through Fornes's workshop, the dramatic centerpiece of the play was inspired by an evening spent with his cousin Grace. Joining them was a similar aged young man who had recently arrived from Hong Kong and who relied on a limousine for transportation. Hwang's initial drafts focused on their ride in the limousine, but two Chinese American literary figures entered into his writing, specifically Fa Mu Lan from Maxine Hong Kingston's *The Woman Warrior,* who is exactly that, a woman who dons the clothes of a warrior in order to avenge the murder of her family, and Gwan Gung from Frank Chin's *Gee, Pop!,* who represents the spirit of Chinese immigrants as well as warriors, writers, and prostitutes. Gwan Gung is also a character in the Chinese epic *Romance of the Three Kingdoms.* The presence of these two mythical figures prompted Hwang to answer the question "What would happen if these two gods met in Torrance, California?"[9] In addition to the autobiographical and literary influences, the play also presents a mash-up of the contemporary American cultural detritus of the late 1970s, as the play contains references to *Saturday Night Fever, Grease,* the distinctive walk of John Travolta, sports cars, and Los Angeles night life. These elements provide a tension for the characters as they must decide between the seductiveness of American popular culture and the trappings of the American dream and the importance of their Chinese heritage and their obligations to familial expectations.

FOB opens with a prelude featuring Dale, an angry ABC ("American-Born Chinese"), who stands before a chalkboard, instructing the audience about the stereotypical characteristics associated with FOBs (immigrants who are "Fresh Off the Boat"). In contrast to Dale are Steve and Grace. Steve, a FOB whose father runs a successful company in Hong Kong, has been sent to study in Los Angeles. Dale's cousin Grace, a first-generation American who immigrated to California when she was ten, attends college and works in her father's Chinese restaurant. The play's first scene occurs between Grace and Steve, as he seeks out a restaurant that serves *bing,* a Chinese pancake. During their conversation he takes on the persona of Gwan Gung, demanding that Grace bestow upon him the proper respect owed to a god. After disabusing him of his ideas about Gwan Gung's importance among Chinese Americans in the United States, Grace in turn invites Steve to join her and Dale for a night on the town. That evening Dale and Steve compete for Grace's attention. Steve, who can speak fluent English, acts like an FOB with poor English skills, fulfilling all of Dale's stereotypes and suspicions about newly arrived immigrants while at the same time besting the

ABC in various competitions for Grace's attention, including a competition of who can best stomach excessive amounts of hot sauce on his food. Grace finally halts their muscle flexing by announcing that they will play Group Story, a game in which all three contribute to the creation of a story. As their narrative develops, Steve takes on his earlier incarnation of Gwan Gung, while Grace becomes Fa Mu Lan, a role she adopted in earlier monologues. Through the battle between these two mythic figures, Hwang not only captures the complexity of Chinese myth and identity but also incorporates the immigrant story of Chinese men like Steve and the generations before him who came to America in hopes of a better future. The play ends with Dale unable to comprehend or appreciate the Chinese and Chinese American experience enacted through Group Story, while Steve and Grace make plans to go out. The final image is of Dale alone with his chalkboard and his cruelly inaccurate characterizations of FOBs.

For a first-time play premiering off-Broadway, *FOB* received fairly complimentary notices from the press. The unnamed reviewer from the *Christian Science Monitor* called the play "sensitive, insightful, and multilevel" as it "joins East and West creatively." In addition, the reviewer noted the ethnic concerns of the play as Hwang "succeeds not only in delineating the differences that separate his characters but has suggested broader problems faced by the Oriental as member of an ethnic minority in the United States." Frank Rich, writing for the *New York Times,* noted that, while the play might feature "unwieldy, at times spotty work," "Mr. Hwang hits home far more often than he misses." He also remarked that the play was beyond a doubt the first "to marry the conventional well-made play to Oriental theater and to mix the sensibilities of Maxine Hong Kingston and Norman Lear." However, the mythical battle of the final act was one aspect that Rich called a "miss," describing it as "a daring gamble that doesn't pay off." While he did acknowledge that the "reconciliation of past and present makes sense intellectually," he stressed that "it has not yet been artfully woven into the body of the play."[10] *FOB* won the Drama Logue Playwriting Award as well as an Obie Award for best play. In addition, John Lone, who played Steve, won an Obie for best actor.

The aesthetic problem of including Eastern elements in a Western play was noticed not just by the newspaper critics. Maxine Hong Kingston, the inspiration behind Fa Mu Lan's inclusion in the play, commented, after seeing the play, that "there's a little bit of borrowing from Chinese theater, but it's not Chinese theater. He's searching, and he hasn't found it yet."[11] Why was the inclusion of Eastern elements problematic? Part of the difficulty stemmed from the play's mythic elements, which originated not only in Eastern sources but also in a Western one. The theatrical movement of Steve and Grace between the contemporary world of Torrance and the mythical world of Fa Mu Lan and Gwan Gung (as well as the inclusion of Chinese immigrant monologues by Steve) actually derived from the influence of Sam Shepard. Hwang was drawn to Shepard "because of the way he juxtaposes reality and myth. He's very conscious that there are links to our past and that we, as a country, have a collective history."[12] Hwang emulated that notion of "collective history" by transforming the characters from present-day college students into mythical Chinese figures, creating "almost a collage effect, bits and pieces of the character at different points, butting up against one another."[13] This fluidity of time and character as well as the inexplicable morphing of a contemporary character into one from the past would continue to be revisited and refined by Hwang in *Family Devotions* and *Rich Relations*. Kimberly Jew remarked upon the confusion that audiences might experience as a result of Hwang's refusal to rely upon the aesthetics of realism on the stage: "These often-surprising character transformations result in several different performance realities and lines of dramatic action, all of which collide in a chaotic, and often confusing, anti-reality in front of the audience."[14] However, Hwang's early experimentation with the fluidity of his character's identities and the blurring of these "performance realities" would eventually coalesce successfully in *M. Butterfly*, contributing to its artistic and commercial success.

On the page the transformational movement of one character into another and back is a simple act of authorial creation, but when one is transferring the concept to stage it is far more complicated, especially when one is dealing with the divergent cultural elements of Eastern storytelling and Western theatrical practices. Hwang discovered firsthand the performance issues when he directed the play and had to stage the extended battle between Gwan Gung and Fu Mu Lan during Group Story. As he finalized his draft, he embraced the inherent theatrical possibilities of incorporating elements of Chinese opera into the work, but as a director he found this extremely problematic since he knew nothing about Chinese opera. Instead, "I went into sort of a ritualistic kind of Sam Shepardy vein where they were just a lot of triangular placements of the three characters with some sort of ritual movement. It wasn't specifically Chinese in any sense, although it could have been somewhat in the sense that it was archetypal enough that it could have been various cultures."[15] Bob Ackerman at the O'Neill workshop provided some initial suggestions about solving some of the Chinese opera production problems, which were then further enhanced at the Public Theater by the director, Mako, who, building upon the Chinese opera component, cast John Lone in the role of Steve, knowing of Lone's proficiency in the genre, since the actor had trained for the Chinese opera as a boy growing up in China. In Mako's production, according to Robert Cooperman, "both Eastern and Western culture occupy the stage at the same time; never does Chinese Opera overshadow Western theatrical practices, but rather blends slowly and effortlessly with them," allowing the Western theatrical elements to serve "as a comfortable reference point for an audience generally unfamiliar with Eastern theatrical customs."[16] This latter point became essential to the success of Hwang's Asian American trilogy, in which he used Western theatrical frameworks that were familiar to his American audience before introducing the play's Eastern elements.

While the East/West theatrical tension has been one of the main points of discussion surrounding the play, the main thematic focus of *FOB* addresses the issue of identity for FOBs and ABCs. The figure at the center of this tension is Grace, who entered the United States when she was ten years old. Her adaptation to her new homeland has been fraught with questions surrounding her identity and placement within American society. Even though, when she started school, she was old enough to be a fourth grader, she was placed in second grade because of her poor English skills. Because she was branded as an FOB during her first year of elementary school, the other Chinese girls refused to talk to her. Grace, tired of being shunned by her own ethnic community, decided that "I had a better chance of getting in with the white kids than with [the Chinese girls], so in junior high, I started bleaching my hair and hanging out at the beach."[17] Her physical appearance, however, made her assimilation into the white kid crowd difficult because, while she could change her hair color, she could not change her skin color or facial features. She was just an Asian face with bleached hair. As a senior in high school, she experienced an epiphany while driving alone though Hollywood. She admitted to herself how lonely she was, and, by acknowledging her loneliness, she could finally see the world around her for what it was, rather than what she wanted it to be. She needed to be true to herself rather than strain to meet the expectations of the larger community.

As the play opens, then, Grace has found a balance between her Eastern heritage and the Western culture that surrounds her, achieving a level of acceptance with herself and her place in life. She works at her father's restaurant, speaks Chinese and English fluently, studies Chinese culture at college, and enjoys the American opportunities and nightlife made available to her in southern California. Her comfort with herself explains her attraction to her alter ego, Fa Mu Lan, who, like Grace, had to discover her own sense of self in a world where her previously established identity no longer existed. Fa Mu Lan's family was killed in an attack; with the slaughter of her family, she was no longer a daughter. Instead, she became a warrior and an avenger, seeking vengeance against the murderer of her family. Fa Mu Lan adapted to her situation, embracing the changes she needed to make rather than fight against them, as Grace eventually learned to do. Both women, through hardships (although Fa Mu Lan's situation is far more devastating), find a proper balance that enables them to exist in a foreign world.

While Grace represents a balanced identity between Eastern and Western influences, Hwang proffers two male characters who have not achieved that same balance. Steve is Eastern based, while Dale has completely assimilated to Western culture. Their interactions with Grace will determine if they too can find a balance between American enticements and their Chinese heritage. Unlike Grace, who engages with her Fa Mu Lan alter ego in monologues, Steve immediately and publicly embraces his Gwan Gung identity. When he first enters the restaurant, he engages Grace as Gwan Gung, asking, "Tell me, how do people think of Gwan Gung in America? Do they shout my name while rushing into battle, or is it too sacred to be used in such ostentatious display?" (13). Grace reveals that in America "no one gives a wipe about you 'round here" (14), except for fifteen students at her college. When Steve surmises that these Chinese students must represent their ethnic group's best and brightest, Grace disabuses him of that notion, admitting that one of the students plans on being a dental technician. Hwang opens with this exchange to point out the lack of investment by Chinese Americans in the mythic history of China. Ban Wang addressed the result of the community's rejection of Gwan Gung and its effect on Steve, arguing that "Much of Steve's estrangement comes from the realization that Gwan Gung is irrelevant here in the United States and that Chinese immigrants are too preoccupied with learning the professional skills needed for survival to care for their own history."[18] Steve conjures Gwan Gung to cope with his own culture shock as well as to probe the importance of Chinese history in his new country as a way to discover a like-minded community. What he discovers, though, in addition to the Chinese American's interest in learning professional skills, is that much of the Chinese community has embraced American cultural totems, such as nightclubs, the Bee Gees, and the films of John Travolta. These items have replaced the stories and myths of their homeland.

Gwan Gung, though, is not the only alter ego that Steve assumes. He also, at various times, takes on the identities of generations of Chinese immigrants who have come to America. Just as Grace's own experience of identity parallels that of Fa Mu Lan, Steve's immigrant experience does not differ from that of earlier generations. Throughout the play, he shares their historical monologues, including one from the early twentieth century, of a man who tried to enter the country five times and was repeatedly returned to China. Despite the continual rejections, he tries again to enter the United States because of the economic difficulties in his village. In another monologue a Chinese laborer is recruited to work in America, being misled into thinking that the country was "a land of gold, a mountain of wealth, a land in which a man can make his fortune and grow without wrinkles into an old age" (37). The frustration of, specifically, Gwan Gung's lack of respect and, more generally, China's dismissal by Chinese Americans as well as the painful travails of Chinese immigration become embodied in a moment of explosive anger for Steve, who articulates both frustrations at once: "I HAVE COME TO THIS LAND TO STUDY! . . . TO STUDY THE ARTS OF WAR, OF LITERATURE, OF RIGHTEOUSNESS! . . . I FOUGHT THE WARS OF THE THREE KINGDOMS! . . . AND THIS LAND IS MINE! IT HAS NO RIGHT TO TREAT ME THIS WAY!" (47). Steve's vituperative response to the world around him represents the multilayered characteristic of the Chinese American identity, which is Hwang's aim. As Kimberly Jew has noted: "Through the character of Steve, Hwang reveals the condition of a splintered and multiplicitous Asian American identity, one that is ruptured by the process of historical immigration" as well as by an ignorance of Chinese mythology.[19] And yet, it is also worth noting, despite Steve's anger, his representations of these immigrant figures introduce a history of the Chinese immigrant that is not widely acknowledged nationally, especially by the Caucasian theater audience and perhaps also by the play's Chinese American audience. His use of this historical introduction works on two different intellectual levels, as noted by Dong: "For the audience who is familiar with Chinese American history, his speech provides enough hints for them to establish a connection between history and reality and to piece together the context. For those who have little knowledge on this subject matter, the play poses a challenge and at the same time intrigues them enough to want to learn more about these historical references and their implications."[20] The lack of acknowledgment of Chinese heritage, then, is combated by the play itself. Hwang deftly raises the specter of historical ignorance as a means to educate his audience.

Despite Steve's sole identification with the importance of the Chinese experience and its history, Grace teaches him to find a balance between the Chinese American community in southern California and his own connection to China. At the play's start Steve searches for *bing,* and he continues to seek it out during the course of the play's action. At the play's end Grace gives him *bing,* which provides closure for both his journey and his relationship with Grace. She tells him: "Eat the *bing.* Hold it in your hands. Your hands . . . are beautiful. Lift it to your mouth. Your mouth . . . is beautiful. Bite it with your teeth. Your teeth . . . are beautiful. Crush it with your tongue. Your tongue . . . is beautiful. Slide it down your throat. Your throat . . . is beautiful." To which Steve responds: "Our hands are beautiful" (49–50). Grace's pacifyingly comforting words ask him to see the internal and external beauty of self. While there is the larger importance of one's ethnic heritage, there is equally an important recognition of one's individuality of self, which is a Western concept. His response to her mantra is telling, as he recognizes his place within the community by his acceptance of the pronoun "our." He has embraced a connection with Grace and recognized his sameness with her and with the Chinese American community. The need to inhabit mythic alter egos or the experiences of immigrants is no longer necessary, as he has now found a connection in this new country. Steve's acceptance into the community that Grace offers suggests an important comment about the immigrant experience and adaptation process. Jew argued that Steve's "ability to embody and articulate a new identity represents a broader and more diverse vision of an emerging Chinese American identity coming into focus."[21] Or, as Gerald Rabkin has suggested, *FOB*, through Steve's acceptance of his new identity, is about "a journey to racial pride."[22]

In contrast to Steve, Dale represents an anti-Chinese sentiment as he proudly announces his complete assimilation to and acceptance of American culture and identity, eschewing his ethnic identity and the heritage of his parents, who immigrated to America. His ignorance of all things Chinese is demonstrated when he asks Grace, "Do you have . . . uh—those burrito things?" She asks whether he means "*Moo-shoo*" (25). Dale's assimilation into Western values leads him to disparage Chinese immigrants, even those only one generation removed from his own status. During his opening lectures on FOBs, he describes them as "Clumsy, ugly, greasy FOB. Loud, stupid, four-eyed FOB. Big feet. Horny. . . . Someone you wouldn't want your sister to marry" (7). His identity as a pure American is self-created and self-suppressed, evidence of his diligence in expunging his Chinese qualities. "I've had to work real hard—real hard—to be myself. To not be Chinese, a yellow, a slant, a gook. To be just a human being, like everyone else" (33). His explicit actions to remove his own ethnic identity highlight his prejudices. He hates his own ethnicity and turns that hate upon new Chinese faces, like Steve's. Upon Steve's arrival at the restaurant, Dale adopts the stereotypical pidgin English of Chinese immigrants to communicate with the FOB: "Your fad-dah tink he sending you here so you get yo' M.B.A., den go back and covuh da world wit' trinkets and beads" (26). Dale dismisses Steve's desire to return to China after graduation, believing the attractiveness of the United States will keep him from returning home. He warns Steve that "you're gonna jump the boat. You're gonna decide you like us. . . .You're gonna decide to become an American" (27). In order to aid Steve, he offers to teach him how to walk like John Travolta, a representative figure of the American male of the late 1970s. When Steve asks why Dale would instruct him in such a manner of walking, Dale hisses, "I'm trying to get you normal!" (34). "Normal" for Dale is everything that Steve is not.

Dale has turned on his Chinese heritage, embracing strictly Western values, not seeing the inherent good that can come from blending the two cultures. James Moy found Dale's attitude to be fraught with stereotype and bigotry, noting that Dale's language mimics the same negative identifications used by nineteenth-century white writers who stereotyped Chinese immigrants. Moy argued that Dale's actions are disturbing because he represents "Chinese Americans overtly disfigure[ing] their own," and that, in giving Dale such power, Hwang has discredited the community of Chinese Americans because the "Anglo-American audience witnesses the establishment of a new order of stereotype, authenticated by its Asian American authorship."[23] According to Moy, Hwang is just as guilty as Dale of using stereotypes. And yet, an alternative reading to Moy's argument exists in Hwang's critical depiction of Dale. While Dale begins the play as an authority figure with his blackboard and educative speech about the intricacies of Chinese American nomenclature, he loses that empowerment through his interactions with Grace and Steve. In a telling monologue that opens the second half of the play, Dale reveals that his anti-Chinese sentiments have left him separated and alone. While he has divested himself of the Chinese American community, he has not been accepted into the non-Chinese American community. He exists in limbo between the two cultures. Lan Dong noted this aspect of Dale's character, arguing that Hwang "portrays his character paradoxically as both a victim as well as a perpetrator of racism."[24] In one monologue he brags about his life and the company he keeps, but his words reveal his own self-created isolation. "I go out now. Lots. I can, anyway. Sometimes I don't ask anyone, so I don't go out. But I could" (33). He also boasts about the number of friends he has, but the number quickly becomes whittled down to one, and even this friendship is questionable. "He has a house up in the Hollywood Hills where I can stand and look down on the lights of L.A. I guess I haven't really been there yet. But I could easily go. I'd just have to ask" (33). Even though Dale has renounced his Chinese heritage, he has not been able to change his appearance, the same problem Grace faced. No matter how American Dale wants to be, he will still display his Asian features; because of his appearance, as Wang argued, "the immigrant cannot simply fit in through outward lifestyle conformism."[25] By the play's end that same loneliness is made manifest as Dale stands before his blackboard with his hatred and racism, instead of being accepted as part of the Chinese American community, the social nexus that Grace and Steve have accepted as part of their own identities, while they eat *bing* together.

Ultimately, Hwang presents a play where complete assimilation is a detriment to a sense of identity and happiness. Dale is uninterested, unwilling, and unable to invest in his Chinese identity, and in return he is left alone, humbled, and uncertain, while Grace and Steve enjoy each other's company. Success—in terms of identity and community—comes to those immigrants and ABCs who are able to navigate the culture of the United States, while also acknowledging and embracing the importance of an ethnic past. Balance is all.

The Dance and the Railroad

For his follow-up to *FOB*, Hwang wanted to write an historical play. He chose to focus on the building of the transcontinental railroad and, more specifically, on a true incident that occurred when Chinese workers went on strike. He chose such a moment in order to disrupt the stigma and historical stereotype usually associated with Chinese railroad workers. He noted: "Most Americans are aware of that the Chinese-Americans worked there, but we tend to have this impression that they were really servile and weak—little coolies who were always being knocked down by big white men on horses."[26] Yasser Selim found this aspect of *The Dance and the Railroad* to be an asset, as Hwang attempted "to rewrite Chinese American history, particularly the railroad workers strike of 1867, from a Chinese point of view. The play celebrates Chinese American solidarity in the face of a capitalistic system that reduces Chinese workers to 'coolies.'"[27]

Hwang centered the play on the character Lone, who has been in the United States for two years, having lost his dream to play Gwan Gung when his parents pulled him out of a school for Chinese opera and forced him to go to America to make money. Once again Sam Shepard inspired Hwang's work, specifically his play *True West,* which features two combative brothers, one a screenwriter and the other a thief, holed up in their mother's kitchen. Each one believes he can do the other's job better, so they switch places; the thief hammers out a screenplay, while the writer steals all the neighborhood toasters. A similar interpersonal conflict occurs in the characterizations of Hwang's play, as Ma, a railroad worker recently arrived from China, believes that, without any formal training, he can play Gwan Gung. His comments lead to a combative relationship between Ma and Lone, which spills over into their respective roles as naïve and experienced Chinese immigrants in America.

After the success of *FOB* and the discovery that they shared similar artistic temperaments, Hwang and two of his collaborators on *FOB*, John Lone and Tzi Ma, reunited for *The Dance and the Railroad*. Lone assumed the mantles of director, choreographer, co-composer, and costar of the production. This collaboration would be instrumental in Hwang's progress in the theatrical blending of East and West, which had been so problematic in *FOB*. Of all of Hwang's productions, *The Dance and the Railroad* was the most fluid in furthering the symbiotic relationship among writer, director, and actors. The characters, after all, are named Lone and Ma, and many of the characterizations and character stories are drawn from the real-life experiences of the performers. Even the actors' vocal inflections influenced Hwang's writing. "I decided to use the real voices of honest-to-goodness Chinese-Americans. The character Lone's voice is similar to the actor Lone's real voice in its syntax and choices of words."[28] Cooperman found the blending of East and West much more successful than in *FOB*, as *The Dance and the Railroad* featured "more of its Asian roots," whereas *FOB* was merely a "Western drama of identity with Chinese opera 'special effects.'"[29] The collaboration among the three theatrical practitioners echoed similar work done by the South African trio of Athol Fugard, John Kani, and Winston Ntshona, who, as playwright and performers, worked fluidly together on *Sizwe Bansi Is Dead* and *The Island*. Whereas Fugard and his collaborators commented upon the political and personal effect of apartheid on black South Africans in the 1970s, Hwang and his collaborators captured the experience of Chinese immigrants in a country that relied on the immigrants' labor for the country's growth but did not accept them as equals. While Hwang would foster strong relationships in the future with such directors as John Dexter and Leigh Silverman and such actors as B. D. Wong and Kathryn Layng, the experience of *The Dance and the Railroad* was unlike any other of his professional collaborations. Hwang explained: "We really worked as a unit. While I don't agree with many people that *Dance and the Railroad* is the strongest work of mine textually, I do think it came off the best because there was a complete integration of text, movement and direction."[30]

The Dance and the Railroad quickly followed *FOB* to the stage, premiering on March 25, 1981, less than a year after *FOB*'s opening at the Public, at the New Federal Theatre, which had commissioned the work from Hwang for its Ethnic Heritage Series. On July 16, 1981, the play transferred off-Broadway to Joe Papp's Public Theater, where it ran for six months. The play was nominated for a New York Drama Desk award for best play and was also filmed and broadcast by ABC television as part of its Theatre in America series.

Hwang did not experience a sophomore slump with the reviews for *The Dance and the Railroad*. John Beaufort from the *Christian Science Monitor* remarked that Hwang successfully continued an element introduced in *FOB*, namely that he has "a particular gift for giving eloquent, comic, and touching expression to the struggles and predicaments of characters who may seem at first remote to the casual playgoer." In addition, "Hwang plays have a poignant immediacy." Frank Rich of the *New York Times* once again praised the originality of Hwang's subject matter and writing, noting that the play featured "Hwang's startling and far-ranging theatrical voice." He was particularly taken with its movement from an "often funny burlesque" to "an underlying sadness," as the two lead characters struggle in a world far different from their own. In addition, he thought the East/West elements worked perfectly in tandem. "Mr. Hwang's works have the verve of well-made American comedies and yet, with little warning, they can bubble over into the mystical rituals of Oriental stagecraft. By at once bringing West and East into conflict and unity, this playwright has found the perfect means to dramatize both the pain and humor of the immigrant experience."[31]

The backstory of *The Dance and the Railroad* is that the Chinese workers for the transcontinental railroad are on strike, seeking fewer hours of work a week and better wages. Rather than explore the economic and political drama of the negotiations between railroad owners and the strikers, Hwang sets the action on a mountainside that overlooks the workers' tent village. It is here that, every day, Lone practices his Chinese opera movements. As the play begins, he finds himself interrupted by Ma, who wants Lone to instruct him in the ways of Chinese opera during the strike so that he can play Gwan Gung. Lone dismisses Ma's request, noting that he himself began studying Gwan Gung only after eight years of practice in a Chinese school for opera performers. Ma persists in asking Lone to teach him Chinese opera, and Lone, worn down, finally accepts him as a pupil. Over their days on the mountainside Lone teaches Ma to be a duck and then later has him hold the pose of a locust throughout the night, while Lone heads down to the camp and learns that the strike has ended; the workers have won many concessions, but not all of their demands have been met. Exalted because of the victory, Lone decides to help Ma become Gwan Gung. Ma, though, believes that his experience of coming to America and working on the railroad merits its own story and is far more pertinent than Gwan Gung's tale. The two then perform an opera of Ma's story, beginning from his forced expulsion by his brothers to a death-filled Pacific crossing to the daily struggles against the relentless mountains. The play ends with Lone continuing his exercises, while Ma returns to camp to prepare for work.

As in *FOB,* Hwang examines the embattled relationship between a Chinese character long in the United States and one recently arrived. In this instance, though, Hwang does not feature economically comfortable college-age characters. Instead, he offers hardworking day laborers, struggling to knock a hole in a mountain. Lone separates himself from his coworkers, working on his Chinese opera exercises while they gamble in camp and brag about how they will spend their money. Each day he goes up the mountain to practice because, unlike his peers, he does not want his muscles to work only for the white men. This sense of self-worth allows him to transcend the pain of practice on top of a grueling day of hitting rock. He tells Ma: "It's ugly to practice when the mountain has turned your muscles to ice. When my body hurts too much to come here, I look at the other Chinamen and think, 'They are dead. Their muscles work only because the white man forces them. I live because I can still force my muscles to work for me.'"[32] Lone's rejection of the West and his affirmation of his Eastern values are physically displayed every day on the mountainside. He has not abandoned China. However, his philosophy of separation did not begin in the United States. In China, Lone's presence in an opera school also separated him from the community. Even though his parents sold him to the school, his presence there kept him from being accepted by the larger populace, as demonstrated by the story Lone tells Ma about the Chinese parents who commit suicide after their son returns home and reveals he has become an actor. Performing is a luxury in a world where laborers are a daily need. Ma's story is contrasted with that of Lone; Ma has adopted the tall tales told to him about the wonders of the Gold Mountain, the Chinese name for America, from the warm snow that his coworkers have described to the vast sums of money he will earn, which will allow him to return home as the village's richest man and acquire multiple wives. Lone's response to Ma's comments is simple: "You are a big dreamer" (61). Ma has not comprehended the truth of their economic predicament—that they must repay their travel cost to America and that the repayments are taken out of their pay, trapping them economically.

While both desire to return home, they see their presence in America differently. Lone is unhappily resigned to his situation, and, while he argues that practicing his opera exercises allows him to control his situation, it also provides him an escape from his predicament. In doing these exercises he is no longer in the mountains of the American West but back in China. Ma, however, warmly embraces the opportunities around him, especially the "can do" mindset of America. Thinking like an American, Ma believes that everything is within his grasp; thus, he asks Lone to teach him opera moves during the strike so that he can then play Gwan Gung. He tells Lone: "Every time I see Gwang Gung, I say, 'Yeah. That's me. The god of fighters. The god of adventurers. We have the same kind of spirit'" (69). Lone, embodying the mindset of China and the importance of tradition, dedication, and lengthy study, scoffs at such a request because of its unconventionality. Training takes time. It is not as simplistic as swinging a pick axe. Lone challenges the strength of Ma's perseverance.

LONE: Could you do it for three years?
MA: Three years? Don't be—
LONE: You couldn't, could you? Could you be a duck for that long? (73)

He believes Ma possesses the same lack of dedication as the Chinese workers in the tent village; he questions Ma: "Yes, but are you willing to sweat after you've finished sweating? Are you willing to come up after you've spent the whole day chipping half an inch off a rock, and punish your body some more?" (65). The most drastic difference between the two men is made clear when Lone reveals, for the first time to anyone, his feelings of betrayal toward his parents who pulled him out of school, sending him to work on the railroad to make money. Ma views Lone's story with more optimism, suggesting that actually Lone has "the best of both worlds" because he can make money on the railroad and then return to China, hire his own opera, and cast himself as the lead. Ma's naiveté infuriates Lone, who responds: "'Best of both worlds.' How can you be such an insect!" (73). In retaliation for failing to recognize his lost dreams, Lone makes Ma hold the pose of an insect overnight, while Lone returns to camp to find out more about the strike.

With the victory of the workers and the concessions they have won from the white owners, Lone's negative perspective about the mindset and mentality of his coworkers changes, and he realizes there is still life in the Chinese worker and reason to believe that America does offer some promise of change and acceptance. Wang noted that the strikers' victory reinforces the importance of ethnic groups to the history and economic growth of the United States: "If a democratic nation takes the principle of citizenship seriously and without hypocrisy, these rights have to be extended to the non-citizens who have contributed to the building of the country. The victory of the strike symbolizes a 're-civilization,' a re-democratization, of the nation-state and reminds the political body of its own principles."[33] Newly excited about his position in this new country, Lone returns to the mountain side to find Ma still in the position of a locust. Ecstatic with the victory, Lone announces that Ma can play Gwan Gung, but the news of the strike's end and his ability to stay crouched like a locust overnight have given Ma a new idea, which reinforces his acceptance of the American value of uniqueness. He turns down the role of Gwan Gung and instead counters with "let's do an opera about *me*" (79). The two then create a Chinese opera, becoming authors rather than just interpreters, documenting Ma's history and creating, according to Wang, "a secular celebration of individual workers and their collective accomplishments."[34] The opera begins with Ma being kicked out of his home by his three older brothers and his ensuing meeting with a white man, who makes false promises about the seductiveness of the Gold Mountain. The story then moves to the Pacific crossing, during which the passengers in steerage struggle to breathe and death comes for some of the travelers. The opera then moves to the railroad and the ensuing daily fight with the mountains as the laborers attempt to craft a tunnel. The mountain strikes back at Ma, hitting him and causing pain. The suffering stops with the struggle of the strike and then the celebration of the workers' victory. Ma wants to end the opera on that victorious moment, but Lone refuses to allow the story to end happily.

MA: Why didn't we just end it with the celebration? Ow! Careful.
LONE: Sorry. But Ma, the celebration's not the end. We're returning to
    work. Today. At dawn. (85)

Instead, Lone, as the mountain, returns and begins to strike Ma, reminding him of the grueling work that awaits them. Whereas the opera element in *FOB* documents the mythic stories of Fa Mu Lan and Gwan Gung, Lone and Ma's autobiographical piece, rather than fostering the larger collective and cultural myths of China, exhibits through Ma's actions the birth of an individual who has faith in himself and his abilities. Ma becomes the author of his own self and, in effect, argues that the individual experience of each man is as valid and important as the myths of old. As Jerry Dickey posited, "Hwang suggests that ancient myths alone do not have meaning for the Chinese in America, but rather the spirit of these myths must be embraced and adapted to the spirit of the modern American warriors."[35] In addition, Hwang's Americanization of the mythic Chinese theatrical form eases a Western audience's acceptance of the unfamiliar material and Eastern theatrical movements and conventions. Cooperman called it "the play's comfort device," allowing "Western audiences to accept alien traditions."[36]

Despite the groundbreaking nature of Ma's individualistic opera, his opinion of his coworkers, like Lone, has changed. For Ma, since the workers did not receive their full demands, the strike was a failure. He tells Lone: "You wanted me to say it before. I can say it now: 'They are dead men.' Their greatest accomplishment was to win a strike that's gotten us nothing" (87). Whereas Lone sees opportunity and the enticing nature of American negotiations, Ma sees only compromise and drudgery for his future in America and wants to return to China as soon as possible. Equally, he now has seen the hopelessness of his situation on the railroad, as the pummeling mountain from the opera has revealed to him the struggles he faces. He moans: "The rock doesn't give in. It's not human. I wanna claw it with my fingers, but that would just rip them up. I wanna throw myself headfirst onto it, but it'd just knock my skull open. The rock would knock my skull open, then just sit there, still, like nothing had happened, like a faceless Buddha" (86). Instead, the strike and the opera have taught him that he no longer can be the naïve man he was during his first four weeks. He needs to be focused and dedicated to the task of returning home, rather than viewing his stint in America as a wondrous adventure: "I've got to change myself. Toughen up. Take no shit. Count my change. Learn to gamble. Learn to win" (87). Ma's comments can be construed as American in principle, but they are now directed toward a rapid return home to China, rather than his remaining in the United States with its unrealistic opportunities for men like him. He realizes that riches are not to be had, since for him America represents only material wealth. In contrast, Lone comes to learn that what he thought was a mere desire for wealth among his coworkers hid a stronger sense of individual achievement and victory against their white oppressors. America, which was once a country of drudgery, has become a place of hope. At the play's end Ma heads off to camp to prepare for work, while Lone remains on the mountainside, still practicing his Chinese opera movements but now possessing a greater understanding of what it means to be an American.

Family Devotions

The final play in Hwang's Asian American trilogy is *Family Devotions*. As in *FOB*, Hwang mines autobiographical material for inspiration. Unlike *FOB*, which was based on an isolated experience, *Family Devotions* stems from a much more personal and intimate part of his life, his family, which would later reappear in various guises in *Rich Relations, Golden Child,* and *Yellow Face*. The main action of the play stems from an incident that occurred shortly after *FOB* finished its run at the Public Theater. Hwang attended a family gathering in honor of a granduncle visiting from China, an uncle the family had not seen for more than twenty years. "We decided that it was important to have a family devotion ceremony and confront him with his past, to see if he could be brought back to God. It seemed really odd, if I put myself in this guy's shoes, that he'd be coming out of the PRC after twenty years and end up in Belair [*sic*] with a bunch of Chinese-Americans playing tennis and trying to convert him to Christianity."[37] The subject of Christianity is an important one for Hwang with regard to the Chinese American community, as he views the Christian faith as an integral part of the assimilation process. By embracing Christianity "you're also taking on what is perceived to be the religion of the society, doing something that's very acceptable by American standards—that is, you're buying into the great American cultural myth, and everybody's very happy. Except for your own soul, everybody wins."[38]

While the play examines the role of Christianity within a Chinese American family, it also fits comfortably into the genre of the American family play. Cooperman described Hwang's entry as "typical American theatrical fare"; however, he differentiated Hwang from those playwrights who had come before by noting that "Hwang does experiment with cultural pluralism by plugging Asian characters into the standard Caucasian American family equation."[39] Standing out from the standard familial equation is the character Robert, drawn from Hwang's own father. Like Henry, Robert was kidnapped, held for ransom, and released. In the play Robert proudly and incessantly regales the family with the saga of his kidnapping and his resulting celebrity status. Hwang's father admitted that after seeing the play, "I felt as if my life had been turned upside down. Of course, if the material is useful to him, he's welcome to it."[40] On the subject of depicting his family members in his plays, especially his father, Hwang admitted: "In terms of my family, I've never felt that bad about exposing family secrets. My dad is essentially of the school that it's better that they write bad things about you than they don't write at all, so I think he's always been kind of pleased no matter how he turns out in the plays."[41]

Hwang dedicated *Family Devotions* to Sam Shepard because the first written pages of the play grew out of a writing exercise led by Shepard—"the exercise was to create a set and then create the characters who lived in that set"[42]—at the Bay Area Playwrights Festival. In addition, Shepard's *Buried Child* influenced Hwang as he wrote *Family Devotions,* as both plays have a mythic sense about them, featuring unexplained occurrences. Whereas Shepard's fictional household is surrounded by a long fallow field that has seemingly overnight grown multiple types of vegetables and, in turn, revealed a long kept family secret, Hwang's household features a grill that suddenly belches forth flames, a tennis ball machine that rapidly dispenses balls with great comedic aim, and the bodily possession of one character by another. Douglas Street noted that Hwang's play also carries some DNA from Shepard's *Curse of the Starving Class,* as both focus on the dysfunctional nature of families and the importance of the American dream and money for the family members. Street posited that in Hwang's play "We watch heritage, values, customs, prejudices as they are batted and battered. As in Shepard, here too there must be casualties. Myths must be ripped apart for the truth to emerge."[43]

Family Devotions opened at the Public Theater on October 18, 1981, three months after *The Dance and the Railroad*'s premiere in the same space. Like Hwang's previous two plays, *Family Devotions* received positive reviews, as the critics appreciated the playwright's comedic presentation of contemporary Chinese American family life. John Beaufort of the *Christian Science Monitor* noted how the play "relishes the Americanized family's assimilation into the ways of microwave ovens, cassette tape players, and other bounties of capitalist consumerism." In addition, the final product "reflects Mr. Hwang's capacity for discerning the universal." However, Beaufort did find the play's Sam Shepard–like ending "baffling." Frank Rich praised Hwang and his playwriting gift, again appreciating the play's combination of American themes and the immigrant experience. Rich wrote: "This playwright crossbreeds sassy, contemporary American comedy with the gripping, mythological stylization of Oriental theater—ending up with a work that remains true to its specific roots even as it speaks to a far wider audience." While he noted that the play is not as successful as *The Dance and the Railroad*, he found it to be one of Hwang's funniest plays. Like the critic for the *Christian Science Monitor*, Rich did not appreciate the play's ending: "Mr. Hwang's extravagant final plot twists get a bit out of hand." Edith Oliver of the *New Yorker* noted that the play was "by far his most complex and fascinating play, and certainly his funniest, compounded of emotion and convictions, irony and humor, shrewdly observed characters, and, as I say, mystery."[44]

The play takes place in the home and backyard of Joanne and Wilbur, a mixed Asian American couple, Wilbur being Japanese and Joanne Chinese. Their daughter Jenny enviously wishes she could emulate her cousin Chester, who is escaping by moving to Boston to join the city's symphony as a violinist. Neither cousin is keen on participating in family activities. Chester's parents are Robert and Hannah, who is Joanne's cousin. Ama, Joanne's mother, and Popo, Hannah's mother, await excitedly the arrival from China of Di-gou, their younger brother, at Joanne and Wilbur's home. When he arrives, after having been missed at the airport by Robert and Hannah, the sisters' most pressing concern, even though they have not seen him for thirty years, is whether or not he still is a Christian.

Ama and Popo's faith drives most of the energy of the play. Their interest in their brother's religious beliefs stems from their childhood, when Di-gou accompanied their most heralded family member, See-goh-poh, on her travels as she converted hundreds of Chinese citizens to Christianity. The sisters are concerned that the Communists may have brainwashed him, taking away his passion for Christ, so they hold a family devotion, in which family members testify about their relationship with Christ, to confirm his faith. After comical devotions by Jenny, Robert, and Wilbur, all of whom fail to display any type of religious passion, the sisters press their brother to admit his devotion to God. When he refuses, they tie him down and beat him. During the beating, Chester enters and is summarily possessed by the voice of Di-gou, who relays the truth behind the evangelical journeys of See-goh-poh. In actuality, she converted no one. She originally went away because she wanted to keep her pregnancy secret from her family. Her subsequent travels were to visit her son, and she covered her absence with the lies of her prodigious conversion ability. When they discover the apocryphal nature of the family's most important moment, Ama and Popo die, as all they have held dear for so many years was false. The play ends with Di-gou leaving the house to explore America.

One common element among the plays in his trilogy is the Chinese American view of America. All three plays feature a character who espouses the wonders of America. Where Dale and Ma were the earlier fans of the United States, in *Family Devotions* it is Robert. However, Robert's view is the crassest of the three, as he is consumed by celebrity and affluence. He believes that only immigrants can truly appreciate the wonder of America because, as outsiders, they can see its opportunities. In a sense, Robert is correct because with distance can come clarity, while familiarity can breed a lack of appreciation. However, Hwang quickly disabuses the audience of Robert's seemingly prescient view of America through Robert's narrow focus on the importance of the self and self-marketing. He has a local newspaper publish a story about Chester's opportunity with the symphony orchestra in Boston. All the information about his son is inaccurate, but the laudatory information about him and his bank are impeccably correct. Robert's decision to become an American was not based on the usual definitions associated with freedom and opportunity. Instead, he had his own interpretation of those concepts, telling Di-gou: "I was just an FOB. This American girl—she talked to me—asked me out—kissed me on the first date—and I thought, 'Land of Opportunity!' Anyway, I decided to turn my back on China."[45] Essentially, he overthrows his connection with his homeland and family because of a first-date kiss. Reinforcing his shallow understanding of being an American, he announces that while America is an easy place to make money, "What's hard is to become . . . a celebrity" (136). And for him the way to celebrity is through his kidnapping. Once again he proffers an unexpected reading of his experience. Rather than viewing his abduction as traumatic and dangerous, he instead praises the opportunity it presents, seeing it as the perfect embodiment of "The American Dream. From rags to kidnap victim" (139). Robert equally worships consumption, arguing that waste is an integral part of America. To prove his point he throws the food prepared for Di-gou's visit onto the floor and smashes it with his feet, telling the visitor: "Us Chinese, we love to eat, right? Well, here in America, we can be pigs!" (120). His view of America supersedes the parameters of Hwang's earlier plays. The self-centered perspective of the college-age Dale and the naiveté of Ma pale in comparison to Robert's stark misreading of American opportunity.

In *Family Devotions* Ama and Popo, two of Hwang's funniest characters, are the main constructors of familial identities. Being the family matriarchs, they have specific perspectives on each member's role with regard to proper behavior and the fulfillment of the family's expectations. For example, their perspectives on Jenny and Chester differ. While Chester's departure for Boston to be a violinist is acceptable, even though he will play for a Japanese conductor, their expectations for Jenny are stricter. At first they tell her that "you marry anyone you like" (103), as long he is a Chinese Christian who graduated from Princeton or Harvard and is a surgeon or a lawyer. When she protests that she does not want to be married but instead wants to be a dancer, they correct her, telling her she has to be a dental technician. They eventually compromise, deciding that she can "Be first dancing dental technician" (104). While their expectations for their grandchildren follow stereotypical outlooks for male and female children, they have a narrower view of Joanne's husband, Wilbur. Since he is Japanese, they do not trust him, as he, in their eyes, embodies all the historical atrocities committed by the Japanese toward the Chinese. Even though he respects both women and treats them with kindness, he never realizes that they make accusatory statements in Chinese about his evilness. For them, he can never be one with their family. He will always be an outsider.

However, while Ama and Popo classify everyone into limited categories, Hwang's play argues against that limited viewpoint, suggesting that a single classification is not accurate, as it limits the parameters of a person's identity. Hwang, instead, offers a variety of types that overlap the numerous characters, including Japanese American, Chinese American, Chinese immigrant, ABC, Christian, Communist, celebrity, husband, wife, brother, cousin, daughter, son, father, and mother. All the characters embody more than one classification, suggesting the complex nature of identity in the context of the various faces that we inhabit. A perfect example of that constant shift of identity can be found in the youngest generation. Jenny and Chester are presented as out of touch with their elders and with their Chinese heritage. This disconnect becomes clear as they try to remember the name of their visitor.

JENNY: They'll expect you to be here when that Chinese guy gets here. What's his name? Dar-gwo?
CHESTER: I dunno. Dah-gim?
JENNY: Doo-goo? Something. (97)

Their investment in their familial past is not important because they have assimilated comfortably into their American way of life. Jenny would rather hide in her room and read fashion magazines featuring Caucasian models on their covers than interact with Di-gou, while Chester is, for all intents and purposes, running away from his family because of their embarrassing behavior.

And yet, despite Chester's desire to avoid his family, Di-gou teaches Chester about the significance of his own role in his family and its long heritage. As the two of them examine the back of Chester's violin, the finish reflects their faces. Even though Chester can run away from his family, he can never run away from his face and, in turn, the connection with not only his immediate family but also his ancestors. Di-gou instructs him: "Study your face and you will see—the shape of your face is the shape of faces back many generations—across an ocean, in another soil. You must become one with your family before you can hope to live away from it" (126). Di-gou's physical and familial connection with Chester is critical to Hwang's larger point about identity. Hwang uses the connection between the two men of different generations, backgrounds, economic positions, and nationalities to show that, unlike Robert's American crassness and Ama and Popo's narrow definition of identity, all of which promote divisiveness, opportunities exist for the expansion of identity, rather than the contraction of it. Di-gou suggests that there is something greater and more significant than a mere focus on the self: the importance of one's historical, physical, ethnic, and cultural linkage. Di-gou's words illuminate for Chester what Ama and Popo fail to see in their sole worship of See-goh-poh, the aunt who claimed to convert others to Christianity. No one else in the family holds the same stature for them. Di-gou's instructions highlight equally all the family members who came before in China, asserting the importance of equality among all the family members rather than the deification of just one.

The conversation between Di-gou and Chester is significant in understanding Chester's later possession by Di-gou, and it is this scene that caused such consternation for the reviewers. Because of their reflected connection on the back of Chester's violin as well as Chester's openness to the deepness of his historical familial pool, Di-gou and Chester become linked, allowing the visitor's voice to emanate through his grandnephew, while he is held down and beaten by his sisters. They have become one as they share the same face, lineage, and genetic makeup. Hwang reinforces the innate interchangeability of the two characters by opening the play with a lone spotlight on just Di-gou's face and ending the play with a lone spotlight on Chester's face as he stands in the exact same spot on stage where Di-gou stood. The visual book-ending of these two characters is Hwang's nod to their intrinsic, inescapable connection. While realistically the scenario of possession is, no doubt, a problematic one for an audience to accept, the inherent theatricality of the scene is believably established through the connection between the two men.

Finally, Ama and Popo's deaths signify that the perception of how they have lived their lives and controlled their family has been founded upon a lie. By deifying their aunt, they failed to open themselves up to the world. The contrast between Di-gou and his sisters is dramatic as Ama and Popo, after years in America, continue to speak pidgin English, live with their daughters, and commiserate over their unhappiness with their respective sons-in-law. In contrast, Di-gou, who has lived in China except for a brief time in the United States, speaks perfect English, is self-independent, and embraces the opportunity to visit America. With the death of his sisters, he no longer is bound by immediate family. He leaves the house with plans to drive a sports car down the interstate, suggesting his openness to exploring the world before him. While Hwang's intention in the play's ending was to use Ama and Popo's deaths to critique the zealotry present in fundamentalist religion, one can also view their deaths as related to the idea of family connections and the importance of ancestry. While Di-gou successfully educates Chester, he is not so successful with his sisters as he warns them, "You do not know your past" (146) and tries to help them see the same lesson he gave to Chester: "The stories written on your face are the ones you must believe" (148). Their limited focus ultimately dooms them to their fate. Like Hwang's previous two plays, *Family Devotions* posits that balance is crucial in maintaining one's identity and maintaining a successful position in the world. Di-gou manages to balance his ties to family, country, and ancestry. His sisters, though, are far too zealous about connecting their identities solely with See-goh-poh. Their failure to find a balance in their lives leads to their ultimate disassociation from society and their family. Luckily for Chester, Di-gou's words help the young man to realize the importance of that balance when it comes to one's immediate, extended, and ancestral family.

CHAPTER 3

Two Experiments

Sound and Beauty and *Rich Relations*

After finishing his Asian American trilogy, Hwang suddenly found himself boxed in by Asian American subject matter as well as by audience expectations surrounding the content of his plays. He noted that "I had exhausted what I wanted to say about what it meant to be an Asian living in this country, the whole ethnicity of that. It was time to move on and see what else interested me."[1] He also found that his philosophy about ethnic identity was not as liberating a topic as he had once believed: "I became aware that there were certain limitations in the sort of isolationist/nationalist models."[2] His next two plays would provide him with different narrative frameworks and subject matters to explore. While neither work would be as successful as each play in his Asian American trilogy, his broadening of his writing style and his thematic focus would be essential to his continuing development as a playwright.

Sound and Beauty

Hwang's next work was *Sound and Beauty,* which is composed of two one-act plays, *The Sound of a Voice* and *The House of Sleeping Beauties,* both strikingly different from their trilogy predecessors. Rather than mining autobiographical material or Chinese American history, Hwang shifted his focus to Japan, drawing inspiration from Japanese artists, writers, and filmmakers. At Stanford, as a student of Asian studies, Hwang found that his interest in Japan was piqued. He was drawn to Japanese culture, especially the work of contemporary writers and filmmakers. Hwang revealed that his "Japanese plays are obviously really influenced by [Yasunari] Kawabata and

[Yukio] Mishima as well as [Masahiro] Shinoda's movies."[3] In addition, he noted the importance of the filmmaker Nagisa Oshima's *Empire of Passion* and *In the Realm of the Senses*. Of the two one-acts, *The Sound of a Voice* draws its dramatic tenor from the structure and characterizations found in Japanese ghost stories, such as Lafcadio Hearn's *Kwaidan*. Hwang found them appealing to emulate because they contain "an element of tragic love, erotic undertones and often a sense of ambiguity as to whether the characters are humans or spirits."[4] Miseong Woo has argued that the play also in some ways resembles ghost stories from Korea: "where a woman turns into a fox with nine tales, the woman character in *The Sound of A Voice* partly resembles the wily *Kitsune,* or fox spirit, who tricks its human victims by toying with their sexual desire."[5] *The House of the Sleeping Beauties* is based on a novella of the same name written by Kawabata in 1961. Hwang, though, took the liberty of making Kawabata a character in his play and included the author's suicide as part of the story, even though Kawabata died in 1972, eleven years after his *The House of the Sleeping Beauties* was published.

In addition to the Japanese influences, Hwang also acknowledged Western influences, particularly Samuel Beckett and Harold Pinter. The plays not only share a Beckettian sparseness in design and atmosphere but also rely on an overpowering stillness endemic to Beckett's plays. In addition, memory plays an integral part in his *The House of the Sleeping Beauties,* suggesting an overlap with Beckett's *Krapp's Last Tape.* Finally, Hwang also noted Harold Pinter's influence in *The Sound of a Voice,* as it relies on silence and an impending sense of menace.

Hwang's writing in these two plays differs dramatically from his style in his previous work, as his comedic one-liners and exploration of the experience of America are absent. These two one-acts are sedately quiet, offering an introspective tone and featuring spare dialogue and characterization. However, he has not completely abandoned elements from his earlier works. Douglas Street recognized some of Hwang's previous conventions mixed in among the new ones in *Sound and Beauty*: "The dramatist has returned to a favorite theme, the relationship of myth and the supernatural to our waking world, but the approach and the vehicle are decidedly new."[6] Robert Cooperman viewed Hwang's movement into Japanese-inspired plays as an important moment in terms of his theatrical negotiations with his primarily Caucasian audiences. "This time Hwang is not shaping Asian theatre around Western subject matter as he did in his earlier work. Instead, these plays show the playwright experimenting with a form which greatly interests him and with which he feels no compulsion to provide Western audiences with comfortable reference points."[7] Woo, though, contradicted Cooperman's opinion about the availability of the play's subject matter for Caucasian audiences, suggesting that Hwang was still writing with them in mind as "the whole aesthetic strategy is geared toward an Anglo-American audience who might just enjoy it as fascinating and exotic Asian ghost stories with trendy music and nascent minimalist set design."[8]

Once again, Hwang and John Lone were reunited, but this time Lone was supposed to be only the director, a change from his multitasking involvement with *The Dance and the Railroad*. However, during the casting period for *The Sound of a Voice,* Lone was almost recruited to play the female role of the witch, since he had played female roles in China; however, the producers finally located an actress who could meet the specifications of the character. Even though Lone escaped playing the witch role, he still ended up appearing in his third Hwang play, playing the warrior in *The Sound of a Voice* after the original actor was fired. The collaboration once again proved that Lone and Hwang shared a common artistic vision, and Hwang trusted Lone to transfer his words and images fluidly to the stage. Hwang remarked, "It's one thing to put it on paper, another to realize it in theatrical form. What John has made possible is for me to physicalize a relationship between the two cultures" of Western playmaking and Eastern theatricalization.[9]

Two years passed between the premiere of *Family Devotions* and that of *Sound and Beauty,* which opened at the Public Theater on November 18, 1983. John Simon reviewed the production for *New York* and had different reactions to each one-act. He found *The House of Sleep Beauties* to be the lesser of the two, noting that the play "could have been moving stuff in the hands of a playwright with deeper, mellower understanding than Hwang, at 26, could come by." In contrast, *The Sound of a Voice* was a far more polished piece, and with it "the young playwright comes significantly closer to perfect pitch." Frank Rich, who had been so supportive of Hwang's Asian American trilogy, appreciated the effort by the young playwright to be adventurous, but ultimately he did not find the two one-acts successful, precisely because Hwang's desire to explore new territory blatantly bled through the material. "Hwang willfully constricts his sensibility into an ascetic esthetic mode: We're keenly conscious of his efforts to duplicate the mood of Japanese literature and theater. The spare visual and verbal brushstrokes are so artfully applied that effects intended as simple and delicate can come across as synthetic and laborious." Ultimately, though, he did not dismiss the importance of Hwang's experimentation with new material, noting that it was "an earnest, considered experiment furthering an exceptional young writer's process of growth."[10]

The Sound of a Voice tells the story of a warrior, who comes across Hanako's small house in the middle of the woods, days from any other people. The warrior's presence there is not accidental, as he has come to slay her, having heard that she is a witch. She invites him to stay with her, and he accepts. During his stay, the two talk and begin to grow closer. At night she plays music to aid him in falling asleep. However, he discovers that beneath her slight, modest appearance she has many skills, including a familiarity with weapons that surpasses his own. One night, upon hearing her play the flute, he peeks into her room and discovers that she has been transformed into a beautiful young woman. Drawn to Hanako, he is unable to kill her. He decides to leave her, and she, feeling rejected by his decision, hangs herself. Immediately after leaving, he changes his mind and returns to her, only to discover her dead body.

In *The Sound of a Voice* both characters feel an inescapable and overwhelming sense of loneliness. Both are loners by nature, one being a hermit and the other a warrior. Hanako's loneliness is driven by her isolated location. Her sense of time completely vanishes when no one shares her home with her. When the warrior asks about the last time she had a visitor, she remarks, "I lose track. Perhaps five months ago, perhaps ten years, perhaps yesterday. I don't consider time when there is no voice in the air. It's pointless. Time begins with the entrance of a visitor, and ends with his exit."[11] Without the presence of someone else, she enters a state of limbo, a liminal state where she exists between time, relationships, and even a consciousness of her current state. In essence, her definition of self exists only through the presence of another, more specifically through the presence of a man. Without her binary opposite, she ceases to have a reason for existing. However, mere presence does not by itself assuage her solitude. Instead, the sound that emanates from her guest provides the comfort she seeks. After the man compliments her on the tea she has made, she responds: "You are reckless in your flattery, sir. But anything you say, I will enjoy hearing. It's not even the words. It's the sound of a voice, the way it moves through the air" (156). Her reliance on the aural to regain her identity and self is Hwang playing with the Beckettian concept of self-awareness. In the Beckettian world a character's existence is reified through a visual confirmation of the self. In other words, how do we know whether we actually exist, if our existence is not confirmed by others? This idea appears in *Waiting for Godot* when Vladimir pleads with Godot's message boy to acknowledge that he has seen him, Vladimir, the next time that they meet. As well, in *Play* M asks the "hellish-half-light," which continually probes him to tell his story, to confirm that he is "as much as . . . being seen."[12] In this Japanese woods, though, the existence of self is defined not through the nature of seeing but through the power of sound and, more specifically, the voice. Hearing another voice or a sound allows for the recognition of one's own self, providing comfort and dissipating one's loneliness.

While Hanako yearns to hear the voice or even the breathing of another human, the warrior too looks for ways to battle his loneliness, especially since he is from the city, where sound is a constant. As he made his way through the woods, he too was overcome by the power of silence and sought a noisy place to sleep before he arrived at her home. He tells Hanako that he slept "by a waterfall. The sound of the water put me to sleep. It rumbled like the sounds of a city. You see, I can't sleep in too much silence. It scares me. It makes me feel that I have no control over what is about to happen" (156). No doubt, the overbearing fear of silence of the characters is of a piece with their fear of death, but for them it also indicates an absence, solitude, and removal from the society of others. Hanako speaks of this aspect with regard to her fear of silence when she explains why she plays her flute at night: "I usually don't play for visitors. It's so . . . I'm not sure. I developed it—all by myself—in times when I was alone. I heard nothing. . . . The air began to be oppressive—stale. So I learned to play *shakuhatchi*. I learned to make sounds on it. I tried to make these sounds resemble the human voice. The *shakuhatchi* became my weapon. It kept me from choking on many a silent evening" (163). As the warrior is able to trick himself into believing he is back in the city by hearing the sound of a waterfall, Hanako manages to accomplish a similar goal with her flute, not only making music but also crafting human-like tones from the instrument to convince herself that she is not alone.

Both of Hwang's Japanese plays focus on the antagonistic nature of male/female relationships, but they offer differing perspectives on the state of how men and women interact and rely on each other. In *The Sound of a Voice* the male/female relationship is embedded in two contradictory aspects that are never reconciled, thus ending in unhappiness for Hanako, with her suicide, and the warrior, who finds her body and realizes that he caused her death. While in a male/female relationship there is a need to trust the other for comfort, companionship, and support, conversely there is a mutual distrust and innate antagonism between men and women, both of which the play explores from its opening. Upon the arrival of the warrior, Hanako immediately invites him to stay with her and dine. However, when she asks the warrior his name, he refuses to tell her, saying that whatever name he gave her would not be his true one. She responds by saying that he can call her Hanako, but the nature of her response—"It's what you can call me" (157) rather than "my name is"—suggests uncertainty as to whether Hanako is actually her name. This strained nature of male/female interpersonal communication was inspired by Hwang's own personal situation at the time. He admitted that he wrote *The Sound of a Voice* when he was "very pessimistic about the state of male-female relationships. I think there's a sense in it of an almost inherent mistrust between the man and the woman, which symbolizes the way, in general, we don't really know one another."[13] The plot of the story supports Hwang's contention. After all, the man's mission is to kill Hanako, whose witch identity embodies the stereotyped depiction of women as evil. Gerald Rabkin, though, offered a differing perspective on the state of the relationship between the two characters. He suggested that Hwang's "inspiration in *The Sound of a Voice* was to write a modern Noh play that challenges this traditional demonology" of the woman as evil.[14] Rabkin saw Hwang's play as undermining this misogynistic perspective. Hanako is not evil but good, and Hwang offers "a feminist theme: that man's fear of woman diminishes his own humanity."[15] According to Rabkin's argument, Hwang's play actually manages to make concord out of the gender-relationship discord.

The ambiguity of the text, though, because of its spare dialogue and character development, allows for a variety of interpretations with regard to the relationship between the warrior and Hanako, especially when one asks: who is the oppressor and who is the victim? Hanako makes a speech that suggests she has always been treated poorly. She describes to the warrior the scope of men's visits to and eventual departures from her home in the woods. "They say they'll stay. And they do. For a while. Until they see too much. Or they learn something new. There are boundaries outside of which visitors do not want to see me step. Only who knows what those boundaries are? Not I. They change with every visitor. You have to be careful not to cross them, but you never know where they are. And one day, inevitably, you step outside the lines. The visitor knows. You don't. You didn't know that you'd done anything different. You thought it was just another part of you. The visitor sneaks away. The next day, you learn that you had stepped outside his heart" (168). From Hanako's perspective the male visitor has caused the difficulties and disrupted the complacency of their relationship precisely because he has expectations of her that are not articulated. When she disrupts the man's expected view of her by being herself, the relationship fails. For her, relationships are destined to fail precisely because of the men's narrow view of a woman's role. She is not allowed to be her true self. Instead, she is expected to adhere to an unspoken, predetermined mode of behavior. At some point, she will disappoint her male visitor without even knowing when she does so.

Hanako clearly views herself as the oppressed one in the relationship. In continuing with this reading, Woo argued that the warrior oppresses Hanako. One of the prevalent images in the play is a bunch of flowers, which do not grow in the area and inexplicably remain blooming even though they should have wilted long ago. In a fit of pique the warrior grabs one of the flowers, throwing it to the ground. Woo wrote: "If the scene is viewed as a patriarchal heterosexual intercourse, after the woman's body is consumed by the man, even metaphorically, through 'looking,' it is wilted and is not attractive to the man anymore."[16] With this reading of play, the man's need to physically interact with the woman is followed shortly by her destruction.

In contrast to such a reading, Hanako can also be seen as a strong character both psychologically and physically. She has the power to control the warrior through the music she plays for him every night, telling him that the act itself "will make me feel . . . like I'm shaping your dreams" (165). At one point when he practices with his weapon, the two engage in some playful sparring, which she wins. She then demonstrates her prowess with a weapon that far exceeds his own abilities. Such an act read through a sexual lens indicates her ability not only to control but also to wield the phallic object, thereby neutering the warrior, physically, professionally, and sexually. Such a reading of strength in Hanako has been posited by Kimberly Jew, who remarked that Hanako has "an intense emotional hunger, a longing that shapes her feminine identity into a vampire that feeds on male companionship."[17] This idea of consumption manifests itself during the sparring scene as Hwang's stage directions indicate that, while the male's spirit is willing to practice, his body is languid in completing the exercises. Over the course of the play the warrior complains of becoming weaker and weaker. Jew viewed this loss of energy as part of Hanako's self-serving consumption: "For as Hanako feeds on the presence of her male visitor and blossoms into her more beautiful self, she consumes his energy, leaving him paralyzed and unable to act. Most importantly, Hanako's feminine multiplicity directly attacks the Man's masculinity."[18] At the end of the play the man's own words support Jew's thesis as he tells Hanako: "Weakness. All weakness. Too weak to kill you. Too weak to kill myself. Too weak to do anything but sneak away in shame" (173). The oppressor in this reading of the relationship is the woman, while the man loses virility, power, and control.

No matter which sex one sees as the oppressor and which the victim, the play ends in tragedy for the couple, brought on either by the warrior's impetuousness with regard to their relationship or by the woman's desperate craving for the man's energy. The man, whether bested by her, disappointed in her, or disappointed in his own actions, decides to leave, just as Hanako has predicted. Her words in the final scene bring the work back to the larger theme of loneliness and the importance of companionship: "All I wanted was an escape—for both of us. The sound of a human voice—the simplest thing to find, and the hardest to hold on to" (175). Ultimately, no matter how one reads the actions of the two characters, the desperation and disappointment of loneliness continue on for the warrior after Hanako's death and, in a larger sense, in all other male-female couplings, which, according to this tale, are doomed never to succeed.

Hwang continued to explore the dynamics of male/female relationships in the companion play *The House of the Sleeping Beauties*, connecting the two plays through what Jew called "the entangling relationships of mutual destruction."[19] In *The House of Sleeping Beauties*, the author Kawabata, an elderly man, comes to a business run by an old woman where older men sleep (and only sleep) with young naked women, both drugged into a state of somnolence. Hwang, though, never takes the audience into those rooms; instead, the dynamic of the piece occurs in the public meeting room of the house, as Hwang focuses on the relationship between the two older characters and Kawabata's desire to write about what takes place there at night. While the writer and the businesswoman initially distrust each other, over the course of the play they come to trust and respect each other through the sharing of stories about family and self. By the end of the play, Kawabata, having decided to kill himself, trusts the woman to aid him. She pours the poison into his drink and he dies, laying his head on the old woman's chest while she too drinks from the poisoned cup.

The House of the Sleeping Beauties also opens with distrust, antagonism, and animosity between the sexes. Both characters, in nearing the end of their lives, intimately know the inherent difficulties between men and women. When they first meet, neither the female owner of the house nor Kawabata displays any generosity or kindness toward the other. Instead, it is all suspicion. Jew described the two as being "engaged in a gendered power struggle over identity, one that is represented by yet another imbalanced host-guest relationship" just as in *The Sound of a Voice*.[20] The owner of the house of sleeping beauties tells Kawabata: "My experience has taught me that in most cases if you scratch a man you'll find a molester."[21] Her profession no doubt supports her opinion of men. She has created a space filled with rooms of heavily sedated young, virginal women. She rents out the rooms to her older male guests (she refuses to call them customers), who are not allowed to violate the girls. They must only sleep next to them. Her choice of older men is deliberate, as she lowers the potential for molestation because of the implied impotence of her customer base. Even if they wanted to act, they would struggle to so, as Kawabata admits after his first night with one of the sleeping girls. In addition, she drugs the men, but not as heavily as the girls, so they too enter into a state of rest and sleep rather than one of wakefulness and desire. The nature of the relationship she creates is then entirely predicated on the need for the comfort that comes from the presence of another, similar to the desire of Hanako and the warrior for the sound of a voice. Here the men long for the warmth of a body. Her business sense echoes her viewpoint about male/female dynamics—the only way men and women can coexist successfully is when both are asleep.

Kawabata, too, has preconceived notions about the nature of the male/female dynamic. His disdain toward the woman who runs the establishment is readily apparent, as he shows her no respect, calling her "an old woman" numerous times and dismissing her perspectives and ideas because of her age. He sees little value in her. Instead, his position is imbued with his own sense of self-importance, based on his belief in his distinction from other men because he is an artist; as he tells her, "You assume that my presence here identifies me as just one type of man" (183). When she continues to press Kawabata, insisting that he desires to sleep with one of her girls, he disabuses her of that notion, asking, offended, "Is that what you think? That I look like a man who goes to brothels?" (184). His reason for coming to her house is to write a story about this secret enclave of sleeping women. His self-interest in writing such a story takes precedence over the lives of the woman and her girls. His artistic temperament is more important than the damage such a story would do to the woman's livelihood and to her employees. He refuses to acknowledge her plaintive arguments about the importance of secrecy and privacy: "We can't let the outside know we're here. That would mean the end of the house" (192). After all, she argues, "This is my life" (194). The creation of *his* art is more important than the comfort of *her* life.

Despite Kawabata's protestations about not wanting to sleep with one of the woman's beauties, she knows the inclination of men better than he does and proceeds to interview him. This includes playing a game in which they take turns pulling a tile out of a structure without collapsing it. The game becomes symbolic of the larger meaning of the play. As she says, "There are no winners or losers. There is only the tower—intact or collapsed" (187). The tower represents the fragile stability of their lives. A wrong move or action can bring everything crashing down, and both characters have already experienced the same disruptive damage to their fragile existences. The death of Kawabata's wife and the suicide of his friend have affected him gravely, eventually leading him to visit the woman's business. The woman experienced her life-crushing moment when she discovered that her sister, who had been groomed by their parents to be the daughter who catches a rich husband, had committed suicide with her long-time lover, who happened also to be the woman's fiancé. The betrayal she felt by both of them drove her into her current profession. In addition, the tiles represent the preconceived and narrow perceptions that men and women have of each other. As she warns Kawabata: "If you try to force the tiles to be what they're not, the whole thing will come crashing down" (187). Kawabata, though, has already begun to force both of them into incorrect categories from his first entry into her house and, not surprisingly, causes the tiles to come crashing down. After the game, Kawabata changes his mind and decides to try out the sleeping arrangement, but he still keeps up his charade of artistic exploration; he says, "I'm really only curious" (190), refusing to acknowledge his baser instincts and his need for comfort and companionship.

Kawabata's experience with and his reaction to the sleeping woman on his first night in the house only reinforces the older woman's point about the base needs of men with their molester tendencies. When he returns the next day, he reveals what took place when he awoke that morning: "I tried to assault her—yes, it's true, I *tried*. But I'm an honorable man, so don't worry for her" (196). His admission angers the woman, and she is inclined to remove him from her guest list, but what stays her decision is his recounting of how he fell asleep smelling the girl's hair. When pressed as to why he did such a thing, he admitted that the smell reminded him of a lover from thirty years before. Kawabata's honesty impresses her, and she invites him to remain as a guest. For many months, he returns, embracing the opportunity of these nights with the sleeping girls as a reminder of his past experiences with women through his drug-induced dreams. However, after having exhausted his memories, he finds that the nights with the girls no longer placate him. He tells the woman: "As I've slept here, I've grown older. I've seen my sweethearts, my wife, my mistresses, my daughters, until there's only one thing left" (208). He now feels imprisoned, as his thoughts are more drawn to death, "the one thing left," rather than love. Driving the change in his temperament from romance to death and a new preoccupation with suicide is the company he has been keeping at night. Jew argued that "The horror of lying next to a dead female body has poignantly brought home the realization that for the last five months, he has been existing on the border of life and death."[22] Just like *The Sound of a Voice*, *The House of the Sleeping Beauties* offers another example of a liminal space where the characters can escape from the usual expectations and behaviors of society. The woman's house offers a space between the realms of life and death, as the older men and the younger women are both drugged into a state that is beyond just sleep but not yet the canyon of death.

However, that liminal space is not permanent and can be violated, as it is when Kawabata finds that one of the girls in his room has died from too much of the elixir and, more important, when Kawabata convinces the woman to mix poison into the tea she always makes for him. He has finally reached a point where life no longer is a necessity, and the evenings with the sleeping women have helped him embrace the comfort of death. However, Kawabata is unable to kill himself. Instead, he must rely on the help of the woman, who pours the poison for him. Thus, his casual dismissal of her value and importance at the beginning of the play is transformed at the end of the play into a respectful recognition of her. As he approaches his death, he realizes that his attitude toward her was inappropriate, and before he dies he apologizes to her for his self-inflated sense of his created identity. She has taught him who he really is, and he truly is no different from other men: "I believed you when you showed me that I was the same as the rest of them" (212). As perhaps the greatest indication of the change in his attitude, he finally asks for her name, which he has never asked over their several-months-long relationship. She tells him that her name is Michiko, and he asks whether he can lie in her lap as he sleeps into death. Rather than lying next to a naked young woman, Kawabata dies in the arms of a woman his own age with whom, over many months, he has engaged in a long conversation on the nature of life, love, and death. It is with and through her that he has found his true self, rather than trying to regain youth by sleeping next to youth. Michiko's status of "old woman" is no longer a mark against her but instead a mark of familiarity, connection, and comfort. And yet, because he has already sent his story about her establishment into his publisher, Michiko worries about her business and future. The result of his presence has complicated her life, but it also has enriched it. As she tells him, "You've proven to me that you're a thousand times more terrible and wonderful than any of my other guests" (212). However, as he falls into the dark sleep, she too drinks from the poisoned cup, dying next to him. The reason for her death is ambiguous. She seeks it either out of an acceptance of her aging body's fate, a realization of the closeness of death that has been around her for so long, or because she is unwilling to start over when her house is discovered because of the publication of his story. No matter her reason, Hwang ends the second play of *Sound and Beauty* with a man and a woman who have made a connection despite the distrust and antagonism between the sexes. Unlike *The Sound of a Voice*, which ends with the warrior's discovery of Hanako's dead body, reinforcing the damage that men and women do to each other, in *The House of the Sleeping Beauties* there is no victor in the competition but instead an acceptance to share their fate together.

A Coda

Sound and Beauty had two more productions of note after its premiere in 1983. For a performance in 1986 at the Los Angeles Theater Center, Hwang replaced *The House of the Sleeping Beauties* with a non-Japanese piece called *As the Crow Flies*, which was inspired by the relationship among Hwang's grandmother, her African American housekeeper, and the housekeeper's alter ego. *As the Crow Flies* was a peculiar addition to the intentional Japanese aesthetic of *Sound and Beauty* with its spare examinations of male/female relationships in timeless locales. One can only wonder about the odd pairing on the Los Angeles stage of a contemporary piece filled with Hwang's customary one-liners and exaggerated characterizations and a play with the universality of *The Sound of a Voice*. The thematic and aesthetic dissonance no doubt explains why *As the Crow Flies* is not often included as a replacement for *The House of Sleeping Beauties*.

Twenty years after the two one-acts premiered, Hwang returned to them with his long-time collaborator Philip Glass and created an opera of *Sound and Beauty*, making changes to both librettos so that they complemented Glass's music. *The House of Sleeping Beauties* underwent the greatest amount of rewriting as it is a far more dialogue-driven play than the quiet *The Sound of a Voice*, which already had a libretto feel to it in its original state. *The House of Sleeping Beauties* was renamed *Hotel of Dreams*. The opera version of *Sound and Beauty* received its premiere at the American Repertory Theatre in 2003.

Rich Relations

While *Sound and Beauty*'s deviation from Hwang's first three plays was recognized for its importance in the development of the young playwright, Hwang's second experiment and fifth play, *Rich Relations*, would not share the same distinction. Indeed, it would be Hwang's first outright failure. After *Sound and Beauty* he found himself in the midst of an extended bout with writer's block. His marriage to Ophelia Chong, in 1985, however, proved to be an important creative boost, and he wrote the play while in Canada, her home country. *Rich Relations* had its off-Broadway debut on April 21, 1986, at the Second Stage in New York City. Whereas his previous play had been an experimental shift away from Chinese influences, this new play was the first to eschew Asian elements completely. Instead, all of his characters were Caucasian, marking the play as the first time he had created non-Asian characters. His rationale for the alteration to his usual modus operandi was his desire to prove that he could write beyond Asian and Asian American experiences, producing a play free of ethnic issues. Hwang explained that he chose such a dramatic shift because of "my frustration at feeling somewhat boxed-in by the Asian-American topic matter which I had chosen—which I love. I think that all of that is expressed in *Rich Relations* in one way or another. Certainly, the frustration at being boxed-in is expressed in the very choice of the characters."[23]

Unlike the dramatic pieces that make up *Sound and Beauty,* he returned to the comedic and religious dynamics present in *Family Devotions,* specifically focusing on the concept of resurrection. As in *Family Devotions,* he based the characters on his own family. Unlike his other plays that were based on actual events, *Rich Relations* was "not *literally* an autobiographical play, there are events that stand in for other things; I've never been convicted of molesting underage girls. I suppose it was kind of a purging of certain guilts and things and self-accusations."[24] Once again the patriarchal figure of the household resembles Hwang's father in terms of his ambition, business acumen, and individualistic streak. These elements had proved to be successful in Hwang's hands in early incarnations. Why, then, did *Rich Relations* fail? According to Hwang, there were numerous reasons: "I wanted to talk about family matters, some of the spiritual issues in *Family Devotions,* but in terms of a family that can be any color. So we cast it Caucasian and it was extremely successful when we read it. Then a lot happened in production—we lost an actor, that kind of thing. When it was not well received that was a blow, because it was a very personal play, about my coming out of the period of inactivity."[25] However, the failure was also, in one sense, a great relief for Hwang because "Once you fail and you exist, you are aware of who you are. Failure gives you complete freedom just to do whatever you want."[26] Despite the disappointment of *Rich Relations,* he realized that he still wanted to be a writer, and the play's lack of success removed the expectations for his writing that came from his previous successes. He now had carte blanche to broaden his reach. "That's when I first realized that I was really going to be a writer my whole life—and that came from a failure. It was the feeling that I could do this and that I still loved doing it—and that it's not the failure or success of a particular work—though you'd rather have a success—that determines your love for the craft."[27] With this mindset in place, it is not surprising that the follow-up to *Rich Relations* was his breakthrough international hit, *M. Butterfly.*

Frank Rich of the *New York Times,* who had been a big supporter of Hwang's earlier plays, thought that his all-Caucasian play was very similar to his all-Asian plays, since they all shared the same setting of California, a religious focus, and materially obsessed characters. Rich found the repetition problematic, stating that Hwang has "regurgitated his previous work with little fresh inspiration. The results, inevitably, are stale." In addition, the story was "wanly conceived," and the all non-Asian ensemble of characters were "credible but bland." Ultimately, Rich appeared to give Hwang a pass for the play, remarking that *Rich Relations* was "an aberration that a talented writer had to get out of his system." The only notable element of the production, according to Rich, was that it was the first play in New York City to use compact disks as a prop. Douglas Street, one of the first academics to write about Hwang, was also equally dismissive of the play, calling it "a tentative, anemic, and caricatured cousin to" *Family Devotions*. The work was "loaded with loose ends and unrealized potential that, with serious rethinking and rewriting, could become powerful theater."[28]

The play opens with Keith, a debate teacher at a private high school on the East Coast, having returned to his father's posh southern California home in the hills overlooking Los Angeles. His father, Hinson, is a real estate success story and has an obsession with technology, ranging from a television that is also a telephone to spy pens, which he gives to his employees. Hinson's backstory drives much of the play's action. When he was younger, he was pronounced dead after an illness but then came back to life an hour later. The incident has had a significant effect on him and the rest of the family, which plays out during the course of the story. Accompanying Keith to California is Jill, a sixteen-year-old student, one of many with whom he has been sleeping. Feeling guilty about his numerous illicit and illegal dalliances, Keith revealed the truth in a letter to the principal and quit his job, and Jill has run away with him. Completing the cast of characters are Hinson's religious sister, Barbara, who wants her daughter, Marilyn, to marry Keith so that her poorer side of the family can have access to Hinson's riches. When Keith refuses to marry his cousin, Barbara goes out to Hinson's porch and sits on the railing, threatening to kill herself if Keith does not change his mind. Later, Jill, who learns that her parents do not want her to return home, joins her on the ledge. Meanwhile, Marilyn has been watching music videos, looking for the video she made with her former musician boyfriend. Suddenly, the combination television/telephone acts up on her, and the lights go out. When they come back on, Jill has vanished from the railing. A futile search commences for her. While Keith and Hinson continue the search, Barbara and Marilyn engage in a Group Story–like recitation—similar to that in *FOB*—about Hinson's death and rebirth. At the end of the recitation, Barbara pushes Marilyn off the railing, and her daughter hangs suspended in midair before the lights go out again. When they are restored, everything and everyone are back to normal. Jill, Marilyn, and Barbara go out for lunch, leaving Keith and Hinson puzzled and seeking answers as to what has just occurred.

Hinson's resurrection is at the heart of the play's story and thematic direction. As a young man, he was a gangster, involved with drugs, money laundering, and extortion. His family was distraught over the path he had taken, as his father was a pastor and his mother was a faith healer. His career path ran counter to their expectations, which was for him to become a pastor, too. The family prayed for him, specifically for a truck to hit him, so that he would be hospitalized and, while there, have an epiphany that he needed to return to the church. Instead of being hit by a truck, he developed tuberculosis. His family accepted his condition as enough of a sign and promised him that they would pray for him if he rededicated himself to the church. He agreed to their proposal and then died. However, as Hwang explained, this is a play about resurrection, and Hinson inexplicably came back to life. He held true to his word, becoming a pastor for a short period of time, but found that he did not enjoy the religious life. He then went into real estate, where he excelled, and amassed riches. Even though Hinson gave up the church as a profession, he did not relinquish his faith. His annual business statement to clients recounts his incredible resurrection, reading: "With God's help, he rose from the death in 1948 to attend the University of Southern California."[29] And yet, his language attests to the slightly off-kilter nature of his faith, as he believes God's largesse is directed merely toward his success: God raised him from the dead so that he could get an undergraduate degree in order to better himself monetarily. That same sense of self-importance dots his interactions with others. One of his clients in passing has called him a baron of real estate, and now he has placed that title before his name, drawing attention to his stature. He believes his employees are all trying to cheat him and has given each one a spy pen so that he can keep tabs on them (only to discover, with Keith and Jill's assistance, that the pens do not work as either a listening device or a writing instrument). His sister's desire to marry Marilyn to Keith only strokes his ego, as he sees the proposed marriage as a reinforcement of his own financial prowess. In fact, because of his importance, he thinks numerous colleagues want their daughters to marry Keith.

KEITH: You think everyone wants to marry me.
HINSON: They do.
KEITH: So they can be related to you. (219)

Hinson creatively uses the concept of honesty for his own betterment, as well. He believes in and worships shadiness as an integral component of the business world. Point in fact: he is so taken with the Hong Kong salesman who conned him into buying the spy pens that he plans to hire him if he ever opens up an office there. Talent like that, he believes, should be rewarded. However, he does believe in being honest about his shadiness. Keith is stunned when his father reveals that he tells his clients about his dishonesty. Keith asks: "You don't want to tip off your clients, do you?" Hinson responds: "Why not? I want them to know I'm honest. If I'm shady, I tell them—right away" (221). In addition to revealing his shadiness, he also lets his clients know he is a Christian. Why? "They respect me more" (256). His faith becomes a badge that covers his faults. Since he is both honest about his shiftiness and a professed Christian, his clients trust him. With such a skewed sense of business and religious propriety, Hinson reacts to Keith's decision to reveal his lawbreaking actions to his principal in a predictable way: Hinson is angry with his son for telling the truth. Instead, he says, Keith should have kept his dalliances secret; Hinson sees Keith's underage conquests as something of which to be proud rather than ashamed. In turn, Hinson enthusiastically welcomes the runaway Jill into his household. Through Hinson, Hwang continues his criticism, which began in *Family Devotions*, of religion and its misused place in people's lives. Hinson represents a religious hypocrite, who uses faith as a crutch to support his material and professional self rather than to help and support others spiritually and emotionally.

Hinson's hypocrisy is echoed in his sister's church activities. Barbara tells Keith that at every prayer meeting she has the group pray for him. When he thanks her, she replies that he should not be appreciative as all the people who receive prayers are awful people. She explains: "We pray that God will improve the whole lot of you. And we pray for ourselves, too. We pray that next time, we will not enjoy the prayer meeting so much. This is a balanced scheme for prayer" (240). While she is an active church member and prayed devoutly for her brother's recovery when he was younger, her faith is presented as a continuous punchline.

KEITH: I can't believe how blatant you're being in pursuit of his money!
BARBARA: Not blatant. Honest. This is a Biblical virtue. (241)

She, like her brother, is guilty of using religion for her own benefit. However, she admits that she was not always that way. "I was not always so interested in money. I was interested more in the things of God. In magic. In miracles. But too many years have passed. The only magic I see now is in phones without wires, televisions which hear you, and ovens that defrost the chicken in only three minutes. So, I must worship God—but I must believe my eyes as well" (263–64). She sees a loss of faith in the world around her and, like her brother, has become bedazzled by household technological innovations, which have become the new miracles and status symbols of society, replacing the church. As in *Family Devotions,* religion is undermined through the actions of the characters, but, whereas the Christianity espoused by the grandmothers in that play is violent, unforgiving, and dogmatic, in *Rich Relations* religion has lost its power and mystery, becoming, instead, a tool to cleanse as well as justify inappropriate behavior.

Hwang does provide an alternative to Christianity via the nonreligious characters. Jill and Keith first became a couple after an odd phenomenon occurred while they were prepping for a debate. Jill describes the event to Hinson: "The wind blew right through the room. And I pulled him to me in a flash. Then everything that wasn't nailed down flew out the window. I was pulling him back from the storm. All I could hear was the rush of wind, my teeth chattering, and my heart laughing away" (228). As a result of this freak experience of nature, they were drawn together. Neither attributes a religious significance to the bizarre weather event. Instead, the incident occurred, and its oddity is accepted, rather than interpreted and imbued with meaning as the two characters find meaning and faith in each other. For Keith, Jill's belief in him inspired him to admit his criminal relationships. He tells her: "You were the special one. And my life began to change. One by one, the planks I stood on were kicked away. By a turn of your cheek, the curve of your neck. I felt it all giving way. I hated it. So I hated you. But all I could do was call your name as I fell—rising up—falling to places higher than I ever imagined" (251). His description of his character's resurrection stems directly from Jill's presence in his life rather than from any type of religious conversion. Jill expresses a similar idea about the power embedded in the individual in contrast to the monolithic nature of the Christian faith. She tells Keith: "To bring someone back from the dead. It should be something you could do twice before dinner and still have energy for dishes. With just a flick of the wrist. The turn of a sleeve. Like magic. But without magic. With just a look in the right direction" (272). For them, all the power of conversion and the sanctity of faith that is necessary can be found within the boundaries of each other's presence and power.

When Keith was younger, he sought answers to his troubles by placing his ear to the floor, hoping to hear a solution. The first time he enacted this ritual occurred when his mother died (she was hit by the truck prayed for by Hinson's relatives). He was at home alone when, inexplicably, a weather phenomenon similar to what transpired in Jill's dorm room occurred. He tells Jill: "The wind blew right through the house. I looked at the ground, then I put my ear against the floor. I listened and listened until I heard a thud, a banging. My heart jumped, I looked up, and it was my dad—home from work. I asked where she was. And he got on his knees and put his ear to the ground, and he listened, then we listened—together" (238). Like the characters in *The Sound of a Voice*, Keith seeks a sound suggesting a movement, a presence, hoping to hear his mother's footsteps, the sound of a door opening, a slight movement in some part of the house. By listening, he seeks the same resurrection for her that his father experienced. The failure of her rebirth draws Keith away from the church and to his current philosophy of faith in the individual. The play's end echoes that same image described by Keith: father and son crouch on the floor, in the same position, listening, as they attempt to make sense of what transpired on the porch with a disappearing Jill and a levitating Marilyn. Just what knowledge do they hope to acquire in that position? The solution is provided by Marilyn, when she levitates above the porch. She proffers an alternative philosophy to the bankrupt Christian faith of Hinson and Barbara. Her offering is a primordial, base, intrinsically linked sound that runs through all of us. "Behind every noise in the city, every sound we've learned to make, behind the clatter of our streets, the hum of turbines, the roar of electricity—behind all this, there is a constant voice. A voice which carries hope from beyond the grave. It speaks in a fine, clear tone about matters which take our eyes upward—away from things we can touch, away from love made small and powerless. It is a voice which lurks behind every move we make. To listen to it is to rage against the grave, we save our souls, we bring ourselves back from the dead" (270–71).

Ultimately, Hwang posits a world in *Rich Relations* where religion is bereft of purpose and the response is to search inside ourselves to hear the voice guiding us to take the right actions and reawaken from our current materialistic, technology-loving selves. And yet, Hwang's alternative to Christianity is problematic precisely because of the characters who espouse it. Keith is a serial statutory rapist, Jill is a runaway, and Marilyn obsessively watches television. This younger generation lacks gravitas and the strength of character to make such options palatable, as their embrace of such non-Christian thoughts has failed to provide any relief to them. Hwang, then, offers a play that, once again, criticizes Christianity but struggles to offer a resounding, believable, and theatrically successful rejoinder. Rather than clarifying his position, as he does in *Family Devotions* through Di-gou's words of guidance, he muddies it, no doubt contributing to the play's dismal critical and commercial reception.

CHAPTER 4

International Success
M. Butterfly

The failure of *Rich Relations* left Hwang at a low critical point in terms of his writing. However, unbeknownst to him, he would soon find himself propelled to the pinnacle of his decade-old career with his next play, *M. Butterfly*. The inspiration for *M. Butterfly*, still his greatest success and considered by many to be his masterpiece, came from a brief news story, featuring the headline "France Jails 2 in Odd Case of Espionage," that ran in the *New York Times* on May 11, 1986, one month after *Rich Relations* opened. The article detailed a French espionage trial that ended with a surprise twist for everyone involved—except one. In 1964 Bernard Bouriscot, a French diplomat working in France's embassy in China, fell in love with Shi Peipu, a Chinese opera singer. For more than twenty years they engaged in an affair, which started in China and continued in Paris after Bouriscot returned home. During their romance, Bouriscot, at Shi's urging, shared government secrets, which she then passed on to Chinese officials. As they lived together in Paris, their relationship came to the attention of the French government, and, after an investigation, both were charged with espionage. At the trial a surprise twist occurred when Shi revealed that she was not actually a woman but a man. Shocked, Bouriscot claimed that throughout their entire affair he had never suspected that his lover was a man. Both were sentenced to six years' imprisonment for spying, but Shi's sentence was suspended, and he was instructed to leave the country.

While at a dinner party, Hwang first heard about the newspaper story from a friend. His question was the same as everyone else's at the dinner table that night: "How could it have happened? But then on some level it seemed natural to me that it should have happened, that given the degree of misperception generally between East and West and between men and women, it seemed inevitable that a mistake of this magnitude would one day take place."[1] Hwang was immediately inclined to adapt the story for the stage, especially since it contained the tensions between East and West that his Asian American trilogy had explored as well as the strained nature of male/female relationships, which was a prominent theme in *Sound and Beauty*. Equally, this story provided the opportunity to expand his focus on these topics from individualized depictions of Chinese American or Japanese concerns to a wider international context.

His first inclination was to write a musical about the story, but he quickly dismissed that idea because "I wanted to start immediately and not be hampered by the lengthy process of collaboration."[2] In addition, he eschewed doing further research, as he wanted the story to be of his own creation rather than a retelling of Bouriscot's version of events. As excited as he was to begin the writing process, he was hesitant to start until he had discovered a way into the piece as a whole. The moment of epiphany occurred on a drive down Santa Monica Boulevard, in Los Angeles, as he was contemplating the nature of Bouriscot's role in the relationship with his Chinese lover. He asked himself: "'What did Bouriscot think he was getting in this Chinese actress?' The answer came to me clearly: 'He probably thought he had found Madame Butterfly.'"[3] Hwang saw Bouriscot and Pinkerton as similar in many ways. While the story of Madame Butterfly has had many incarnations by Western authors, Giacomo Puccini's version has become the representative model of the doomed relationship. In Puccini's *Madame Butterfly* Pinkerton, an American sailor, marries Cio-Cio San, a young Japanese girl. Shortly after they marry, he leaves her to return to America, and she gives birth to their son in his absence. When he returns, three years later, he arrives with his American wife, who has agreed to raise Cio-Cio's son as her own in America. Cio-Cio relinquishes her son to her husband's Western wife and then commits suicide. Hwang's play would incorporate the opera as an important framework for the telling of the story and the introduction of his characters. The fact that Shi Peipu was an opera performer only reinforced the appropriateness of connecting Puccini's opera to the Chinese–French love affair he was to explore.[4] Having found his inspiration for the overarching narrative for the story, Hwang needed only six weeks to write the play, which he entitled *Monsieur Butterfly*. His wife, Ophelia, noted that the title was too obvious about the Chinese spy's gender and suggested that the title be *M. Butterfly*. Jon Rossini noted the effectively disruptive meaning embedded in such a change, arguing that converting Madame/Monsieur to just the letter

"M" "pulls apart the Orientalist project that the play initially appears to embrace" and in turn "derail[s] the easy assumption of gender."[5]

Hwang shared his script with the producer Stuart Ostrow, who immediately began the process of getting the play staged. Ostrow sent the script to John Dexter, director of the original production of Peter Shaffer's *Equus,* which features the narrative device of a character who tells the story through flashbacks, a technique that Hwang emulates in his play. Hwang has acknowledged that Shaffer's *Amadeus,* which uses a similar narrative device, influenced him. While the format was similar to that of *Equus,* Dexter was drawn to *M. Butterfly* for different reasons: he was impressed with its "language and the freedom with which [Hwang] uses the stage, playing across time, space, geography."[6] Dexter signed on to be the director the day after he finished reading the script. On the basis of the strength of the piece, the producers, which now included the record mogul David Geffen, decided that the play was definite Broadway material. Jack Viertel, one of the play's producers, explained the play's strength in comparison to Hwang's previous work: "It's the first play David's written that deals with history in a way that isn't totally imaginary or imagined; he's using the real world in a highly theatrical way. It's a much larger version of what he was doing in *The Dance and the Railroad*—take an event and find the underlying social and political meaning of it."[7] When the hiring process was complete, John Lithgow had signed on to play Gallimard, the Bouriscot role, and, after six months of auditions, B. D. Wong was cast as Song, the Shi Peipu role.

M. Butterfly is narrated by Gallimard from his French prison cell as he takes the audience through the twenty-year love affair he had with Song Liling, a Chinese opera singer. He first meets her at an embassy party where she sings the love song from *Madame Butterfly* for the assembled diplomats. After revealing her disdain for the untruthfulness of the Puccini story, she invites Gallimard to visit her at the Chinese opera. After he visits, their love affair slowly begins to evolve. Hwang intercuts the developing romance between the two characters with Gallimard's own recitation of his unsuccessful sexual interactions with the opposite sex as he grew up, a time when he had to rely on his friend Marc to help him with his sexual conquests. In addition, he relates his love of Puccini's *Madame Butterfly,* which tells of Pinkerton's ability to exert total control over his Japanese wife. Gallimard assumes the Pinkerton role in his relationship with Song, his Chinese version of Puccini's Cio-Cio San. His newfound position as a sexual conqueror leads to success in the embassy, where he becomes an analyst advising the Americans about invading Vietnam. However, Gallimard's narrative control of his story is sporadically lost as Song takes over, revealing through scenes with a government official, Comrade Chin, that she is a spy for China. Gallimard is eventually sent back to France, and Song is sent after him. Between the second and third acts Song transforms in front of the audience from a woman to a man, switching her garments from a kimono to an expensive Western suit. During the espionage trial, the secret of Song's identity is revealed to the country and the world. Song and Gallimard finally confront each other, and Song undresses, revealing once and for all that he is a man. Gallimard, his fantasy of Song finally destroyed, dons makeup and kimono and kills himself, realizing that he has actually been the Butterfly to Song's Pinkerton.

The producers decided the play would have one tryout period outside New York City and then open on Broadway, making Hwang the first Asian American writer to have a play produced on the Great White Way. While there was excitement about the ascension of Hwang to the status of Broadway playwright and, in turn, about Asian Americans finally having a strong representative theatrical voice, there also was dissatisfaction within the Asian American community about the way Hwang achieved this rarefied status. Esther Lee Kim pointed out that "the most famous Asian American play did not get developed at an Asian American theatre company or receive direct support from the community. Instead, the production's creative team consisted of non-Asian American artists from the mainstream theatre."[8] Kim would not be the only Asian American voice to criticize Hwang's play. In the years after the play's premiere, numerous scholars would publish their concerns about Hwang's depiction of his Asian characters and, in turn, his failure to serve as a constructive voice for the Asian American community. Quentin Lee, a vociferous critic of the play and, even more so, of Hwang, found multiple faults in the play; he said it was not "excessive enough—not subversive enough—not Orientalist enough."[9] In addition, the piece failed because of its "commodifying geographical exoticism (France and China) to appeal to the hybridized American fetish of Occidentalism and Orientalism: France, how classy! China, how exotic!"[10] Williamson Chang acknowledged that while the play depicts an Eastern character who is victorious over the West, Hwang accomplishes this disruption of the Western power ethic through the reification of the usual Asian stereotypes, especially of Asian women, who are portrayed as "cunning, shrewd, manipulative, and deceptive," whereas characters from the West are seen as "trusting, idealistic, misinformed, and generous."[11] Hsiu-Chen Lin argued a similar point about Hwang's complicity in relying upon Asian stereotypes when it comes to Song, whose acceptance of the Eastern stereotype expected of her by her Western lover allows for her victory. After all, at the play's end Gallimard is dead and Song is alive. Song's willingness to embody his fantasy allows Gallimard to attain what he covets, including secrets, love, and fine clothing. However, Lin noted that, despite Song's success, she engages in actions that resemble those of "the Dragon Lady, whose sexual perversion lures innocent white men into danger. Thus Song becomes, more than ever, a stereotypical threat to Western morality and security."[12]

James Moy also criticized the play's stereotypical depiction of its Asian characters, especially Song. *M. Butterfly* "disintegrates, for [Hwang] offers at best another disfigured stereotype" in his presentation of Song.[13] Hwang's Asian creations are "marginalized, desexed and made faceless" in that they pose "no threat to Anglo-American sensibilities" because they exist as "exotic Orientalist fetishes articulating Anglo-American desire," meaning that the intentions of subverting Western sensibilities about the East are undermined via their reification of already established prejudices.[14] Instead of engaging the audience with larger issues concerning gender, East/West relations, and Asian depictions, Hwang shortchanges the audience, which pays scant attention to these larger issues because they are "incredulous at how for twenty years Gallimard could have confused Song's rectum for a woman's vagina."[15] Of all Hwang's works, *M. Butterfly* would generate the greatest number of scholarly reactions.

The out-of-town tryout, in Washington, D. C., was revelatory for Hwang and his creative partners, especially on opening night. Since the play had no significant advance publicity or any buzz surrounding it, the opening-night audience reacted in a manner that, according to Hwang, was unique. In the third act there is a pivotal scene where Song fully disrobes in front of Gallimard, revealing the truth about his sex to his lover. Hwang remarked that "when B. D. Wong dropped his drawers, the audience literally screamed. It was really cool. It was like when Glenn Close came out of the water in *Fatal Attraction*."[16] Because of the immediate success and notoriety of the play and the word of mouth that surrounded the incredible performance by Wong, Hwang noted that opening-night reaction from the audience "has never been duplicated, but I always really treasure it."[17] However, the revelation scene still possessed the power to shock its audience, as noted by Anne Cheng; she saw the play three times during its Broadway run, and "each time the infamously jaded audience of Manhattan still gasped when Song undressed and revealed his masculinity."[18] An element of the production from the opening night that has continued to stay with it is the seduction of not only Gallimard but also the audience into believing Song is a woman.

The program's cast list blurred the identity of the performer playing Song. It listed the performer only as B. D. Wong, allowing an audience member to decide the actor's gender, much like the lone "M" in the play's title.

The power of the performer to convince the audience of Song's femininity is a palpable element of the production's success, and when I saw a touring production of the play in Baltimore in December 1990, audience members were seduced by the performance of A. Mapa, Wong's replacement as Song. An older gentleman behind me refused to believe that a man had played the opera singer in the first two acts of the play. As we left the theater, he continued to argue with his party, asserting that it was a woman who had played Song in the first two acts and a man in the last act. In this case and in many others, the attraction that Gallimard feels toward Song is echoed by the male members of the audience. However, once Song is revealed to be a man, then male audience members enticed by Song in the first two acts suddenly discover they were attracted to a man, an indication of the play's ability to challenge the audience's ideas about gender preferences when it comes to sexuality and seduction. One other element was discovered during the tryout—that the title prompted some confusion. Hwang "overheard a woman say to her husband, 'You said it was going to be *Madame Butterfly,* and there wasn't a single song.'"[19] After its Washington run the play moved to Broadway, opening on March 20, 1988, and costing $1.5 million to produce, making it the most expensive play to open in New York that year.

Frank Rich of the *New York Times* had a decidedly mixed reaction to *M. Butterfly.* He admired the play itself, calling it "a visionary work that bridges the history and culture of two worlds" and a "brilliant play of ideas," but struggled to appreciate the production. He observed that "the experience of seeing the play isn't nearly as exciting as thinking about it after the curtain has gone down." He felt that the production's strongest element was Song's revelation of his true gender. Until that point the audience had had to "settle for being grateful that a play of this ambition has made it to Broadway, and that the director, John Dexter, has realized as much of Mr. Hwang's far-ranging theatricality as he has." One of the most troubling aspects of the production for Rich was Lithgow's unsuccessful interpretation of Gallimard. Rich revisited the play when David Dukes assumed the lead and finally experienced the production he had been craving on opening night. His reassessment of the play noted that Duke's performance transformed the production from an engaging intellectual experience into a powerfully emotional night of theater. John Gross also reviewed the play for the *New York Times,* and while he wrote equally favorably about the play, he noted Hwang's tendency to be overly didactic. Even though he deemed *M. Butterfly* worth seeing, he tempered his recommendation by calling it "a mess, intellectually speaking" and noted that the play "would have been better, in fact, if Mr. Hwang hadn't been tempted to pile on the ideas; if he had kept them, at best, in second place, as implications and overtones. As it is, they clutter up the foreground of the play and seriously coarsen its texture." Like his colleague, Gross did find the transformation scene a particularly powerful theatrical moment. His enthusiasm was echoed by John Beaufort of the *Christian Science Monitor,* who effused that "the final transformation scenes are master strokes of theatrical invention." Finally, Michael Feingold of *The Village Voice* applauded the audacity of the entire concept: "As for the notion that a major Broadway event could be made out of a homosexual love story shot through with social and political ideas—I'm in awe of Hwang and everyone else involved for sticking their necks out so far."[20]

Perhaps one of the strongest and most inaccurate predictions expressed about the play ran in *USA Today,* where Jacques Le Sourd called the play a "Big Broadway Bomb" because it "looks like and sounds like a bad play, a very bad play," citing its overreliance on allegory and on a lead French character who sounds more American than French. Jack Kroll of *Newsweek* shared a similar perspective, remarking that "this butterfly is a paper lepidopteran. Hwang has concocted a play that consumes itself in its own cleverness, that takes so many twists and turns that it spins itself into a brilliant blur." He explained that "at every level the play defies belief" and that, unlike his colleagues, he never believed B. D. Wong was a female and found the transformation scene between the last two acts, in which Song changes from a woman to a man before the audience's eyes, to be interminable. John Simon of *New York* shared similar sentiments, but, unlike his colleagues, he thought the transformation sequence was exceedingly effective, which was precisely the problem. He wrote that "the five minutes during which Song wordlessly removes his female makeup and garb and changes back into a man are among the most theatrically effective; I mistrust a play in which so long an absence of dialogue comes as a relief." In addition, he cited Hwang for "authorial laziness" because of his failure "to explore the deeper workings of the central relationship. For psychology, he often substitutes one-liners and posturing; for tormented poetry, angry rhetoric."[21] Despite the comments of these reviewers,[22] *M. Butterfly* was Hwang's most decorated play, as it was nominated for the Pulitzer Prize and won the Drama Desk Award, Outer Critics Circle Award, and John Gassner Award for best play. The production received seven Tony nominations, winning best director for John Dexter, best play for David Henry Hwang, and best featured actor for B. D. Wong. In 1993 the play was adapted into a film directed by David Cronenberg, starring John Lone and Jeremy Irons, and featuring a screenplay by Hwang.

When I teach *M. Butterfly*, the question about the Bouriscot case is still the most pressing question for students: how could Gallimard not know for twenty years that Song is a man and that he is engaging in a homosexual relationship? Hwang's answer is that Gallimard relies on fantasy to obfuscate the truth of his romantic situation. In numerous interviews Hwang has argued that when we are in a romantic relationship that appears to be perfect, we effectively blind ourselves to the reality and faults of our partner, preferring to see what we want to see rather than acknowledge what is truly there. He admits, though, that while the relationship between Song and Gallimard represents an extreme demonstration of that principle, "it's not actually that different qualitatively from everyday types of deceptions that people make in order to convince themselves they're in love."[23] Throughout the play Hwang builds a convincing case for Gallimard's self-deception about Song's sex. Part of it is driven by Gallimard's own lack of experience in the world of sexual relations. Orgies and naked pool parties thrown by his friend Marc made him hesitant and uncomfortable. His first sexual experience occurred in some dark bushes where he was manhandled by an overactive and loud teenage girl who thought he was somebody else. He came away from the experience completely unimpressed by and actually a bit frightened of sexual intercourse. In addition, girls in magazines left him limp and unengaged, making him wonder, "My skin is hot, but my penis is soft. Why?"[24] His eventual marriage to Helga—the name says it all—is one of convenience rather than romance, and even his extra-extramarital affair (he cheats on Song) with a foreign exchange student is ineffective, as she is too open and revealing, prompting him to wonder: "Is it possible for a woman to be *too* uninhibited, *too* willing, so as to seem almost too . . . masculine?" (54). From these instances, Hwang makes it clear that women, specifically Western women, confuse and scare Gallimard.

Song, though, is neither of these things precisely because she fulfills Gallimard's Puccini-influenced view of Eastern women, and she recognizes this element in Gallimard's character when he first speaks to her about *Madame Butterfly*. She asks him, "It's one of your favorite fantasies, isn't it? The submissive Oriental woman and the cruel white man" (17). With her encouragement, Gallimard embraces the role of the cruel white man and, in turn, believes he has complete power over her. However, moments of doubt about the veracity of her gender do creep into his mind and at one point Gallimard confronts Song, asking her to undress in front of him. Her modesty and shame prevent him from forcing her to disrobe. Afterward, he ponders, "Did I not undress her because I knew, somewhere deep down, what I would find?

Perhaps. Happiness is so rare that our mind can turn somersaults to protect it" (60). In addition, Gallimard embraces the relationship because he sees a bit of himself in Song. As Anne Cheng suggested, "Song provides a mirror image of Gallimard. They are both described as shy, passive, not wanting to undress, etc. Indeed, Song-as-woman very much resembles Gallimard-as-man."[25] With such a connection to Song's persona, Gallimard convinces himself that she is what he thinks she is rather than what she actually is. Ultimately, though, the reality of living a true Pinkerton-and-Butterfly romance supersedes any doubts he might have as to Song's true sexual identity. As Gallimard tells us, "I suggest that, while we may all want to kick Pinkerton, very few of us would pass up the opportunity to *be* Pinkerton" (42). Gallimard's statement is something Hwang sees as being endemic to the male experience as a whole. "The really sexist things Gallimard says are things that I know on some level work in my own soul and color my relationships with women. Pleasure in giving pain to a woman is not that far removed, I think, from a lot of male experiences."[26] Despite Gallimard's behavior toward Song, Hwang's play entices the male audience members to be drawn to Gallimard's superiority in the relationship, something the men in *Sound and Beauty* lacked vis-à-vis their female partners.

Pinkerton's relationship with Cio-Cio San, though, is a heterosexual one, while Gallimard's relationship with Song is a homosexual one, which prompts the question of Gallimard's sexual orientation. Is he hetero- or homosexual? Hwang offers an interesting take on Gallimard's sexuality, suggesting that "I think he knows he's having an affair with a man. Therefore, on some level he is gay."[27] Despite the author's contention that his character is homosexual, scholars offer various interpretations of Gallimard's sexual orientation. David Eng agreed with Hwang's assessment that Gallimard is gay, making his case through Gallimard's sexual deficiencies with the opposite sex when he was a young man. Eng further stated that the Frenchman is actually a closeted homosexual, who constantly requires the socially appropriate appearance of heterosexuality. Thus, he dons a kimono and makeup at the end of the play, becoming the Butterfly of the relationship, because "now that Song is publicly a man, Gallimard must become publicly the woman."[28] By feminizing himself, Eng argued, Gallimard rights the relationship from a homosexual one back to the societally accepted heterosexual one.[29] Dorinne Kondo extended Eng's idea further, focusing on the moment when Song fully reveals himself to Gallimard. She suggested that Song attempts to convince his lover "to join him in a new sort of relationship, where Song is more like a man, Gallimard more like a woman. At precisely this point Hwang suggests the inability of the categories of man and woman to account for the multiple, changing, power-laden identities of his protagonists."[30] The opportunity for a complete redefinition of sexual categorization is rejected by the socially conscious, predetermined, Western mindset of Gallimard. Andrew Shin concurred that Gallimard is a homosexual but argued that Gallimard kills himself "because he can no longer defend against knowledge of his homosexuality in the homophobic West."[31] Josephine Lee, though, posited that Gallimard is actually not a homosexual but instead possesses a fetish for Asian skin, which explains his lack of sexual attraction to his French female classmates and the pin-up girls in the magazines. They all are Western girls, and "the stereotype of the submissive woman as Caucasian is not enough as a fulfilling fiction."[32] For Gallimard, gender is not as important as skin type; "the Asian body itself *is* the fetish, the object of desire."[33]

As Hwang had done before, in *M. Butterfly* he revisits his interest in the conflict between East and West, as embodied in the relationship between Gallimard and Song. However, as Rocio Davis has noted, Gallimard's fantasy of finding a Butterfly to his Pinkerton is problematic in that it colors his understanding of the East as a whole. Davis argued, "Gallimard's fantasy merges the Orient into one indistinguishable mass, eliminating the differences among Chinese, Japanese and Vietnamese."[34] From his first meeting with Song, when he praises her convincing and powerful rendering of Puccini's tragic heroine, he awkwardly lumps disparate Asian countries together, not realizing the inherently problematic nature of a Chinese opera singer playing a Japanese character. Song is offended at his compliment: "Convincing? As a Japanese woman? The Japanese used hundreds of our people for medical experiments during the war, you know. I gather such an irony is lost on you" (17). Later, when he receives his promotion, he is asked for a report about how the Vietnamese would react to the presence of Americans in their country. His entire recommendation reflects his experience with Song, a Chinese woman, as he argues "The Orientals simply want to be associated with whoever shows the most strength and power" (45) and that "Orientals will always submit to a greater force" (46). Not realizing that Song is playing a role when she submits to Gallimard, he is unaware that his understanding of the East is entirely manipulated by her behavior toward him.

Not surprisingly, his recommendations about Americans in Vietnam are completely incorrect, and he is sent back to France. In the French courtroom, Song reveals exactly why the tension and misperception between the East and West exist. He tells the judge during the trial, "As soon as a Western man comes into contact with the East—he's already confused. The West has sort of an international rape mentality towards the East" (82), which is embodied in the *Madame Butterfly* story, in which Pinkerton is free to treat

Cio-Cio San with complete disrespect. The same attitude extends to Western governments' dealings with the East and also extends to the male populace of the West. Song himself has been the victim of the West's superior attitude toward the East. He states to the courtroom, "I am an Oriental. And being an Oriental, I could never be completely a man" (83). His statement is borne out when he confronts Gallimard and strips before him. Gallimard laughs hysterically at the naked Chinese man before him, sending Song scrambling to pick up his suit and reclothe himself. Song's bid to receive the esteem he deserves is met thus with amusement, rather than love and respect.

The revelation of Song's sex forces Gallimard to make a choice about the nature of their relationship in terms of its East/West dynamic, whether to accept the reality of Song's new Western bearing or to maintain his Butterfly fantasy. Gallimard tells Song: "Tonight, I've finally learned to tell fantasy from reality. And, knowing the difference, I choose fantasy" (90). He has become consumed by the fantasy of the strong Western male and his weak, submissive Eastern lover. Seeing Song as a man in Western clothes, Gallimard assumes the identity of the Eastern woman. Jon Rossini argued that as Gallimard's fantasy explodes, it must be righted, so "he attempts to obviate the real gendering of the relationship as problematic by continuing to insist on the presence of Butterfly and protecting this denial through a fantasy of cultural transformation—Gallimard becomes Oriental, at least through his final ritual action of seppuku."[35] His death then reifies his East/West fantasy through his assumption of the role of Butterfly, a role he unknowingly fulfilled throughout his entire affair with Song, who was Pinkerton-like in his control and manipulation of Gallimard. Sherrill Grace suggested a parallel reading to the East/West dynamic of the play's ending, arguing that Gallimard must kill himself because Song's manipulations have made him the female partner in the relationship and, in his Western, white male mindset, "to *be* a woman is a fate worse than death."[36] Along the same lines and considering Song's courtroom observations about Western views of the East, for a Westerner to become an Easterner "is a fate worse than death." Having lost his Western credentials, Gallimard must kill himself. Hsiu-Chen Lin, though, foresaw a problem with Gallimard's assumption of the sympathetic role of Butterfly in the play's last moments as he commits suicide. If the audience sympathizes with Gallimard and empathizes with his death, then, Lin argued, it too has subscribed to and condoned his fantasy about how the East should function in regard to its women, relationships, and the East's political place in the world. The play's attempt, then, to challenge the stereotypical and Western culturally defined prescriptions for the East fails and instead continues to reinforce a prejudicial view of the East through its ending. In contrast, Hwang has suggested that the play's end shows Song's loss of power over Gallimard, who he had in his grasp throughout their relationship. Song believed that once he revealed his true self to Gallimard, the Frenchman would still love him as a man as he had when Song was believed to be a woman. Hwang said that with Gallimard's rejection, Song's "whole bubble of superiority, his whole bubble of, again, male-dominant fantasy, collapses."[37]

As we know, scholars and writers do not always agree on the meaning of a text, and this is true for *M. Butterfly*, which offers many moments of ambiguity and rich material to interpret, prompting scholars to read the play in myriad ways, including the role of transvestism, the power of fantasy, the problematic nature of the play's stereotyping of Asians and females, and the demonstration of Western imperialism. Because of the multilayered quality of the material, *M. Butterfly* is Hwang's most written-about play, accounting for the majority of scholarly work on him. Equally, it is his most often taught work, having achieved canonical status in multiple dramatic literature anthologies as a representative of the best of American, contemporary, and world drama. No doubt, as China's movement toward superpower status solidifies, *M. Butterfly*'s stature will continue to grow given its relevance in challenging assumptions between the East and West.

Hwang and Hollywood

M. Butterfly completely transformed the track of Hwang's career, turning him into an internationally recognized playwright. As is the case for playwrights who become successful on Broadway, Hollywood immediately sought him out. Hwang's screen adaptation of *M. Butterfly* was not his only writing for the screen. In addition to a number of projects that never made it out of preproduction, he wrote the original screenplay *Golden Gate* and an NBC miniseries called *The Lost Empire*, also known as *The Monkey King;* in addition, he cowrote, with Neil LaBute, the screen adaptation of A. S. Byatt's *Possession*. His most recent play, *Chinglish,* was optioned by Hollywood with Hwang attached to write the screenplay. However, the success that Hwang had in the theater has not transferred to the silver screen. The movie version of *M. Butterfly* failed to capture the energy that the play had on the stage and fizzled at the box office. *Golden Gate*, which starred Matt Dillon and Joan Chen, about an FBI agent's involvement with two generations of a Chinese American family, had even less success at the box office than *M. Butterfly. The Lost Empire*, based on the Chinese story *Journey to the West,* premiered at a time when miniseries were waning on network television, and *Possession,* about two academics falling in love while researching two Victorian poets, was anticipated to be a contender for end-of-the-year awards but did not succeed in winning awards or at the box office. Of the wide range of writing opportunities afforded Hwang, including musical books and opera librettos, he has found screenwriting the most difficult in terms of achieving the success he has found through his plays. In 2012 Hwang returned to the movies this time as an executive producer for Quentin Lee's *White Frog*, which also features Hwang as an actor.

CHAPTER 5

After *M. Butterfly*
Controversy, Love, Failure, and Gold

The transfer of a hit West End musical to Broadway would frame much of Hwang's dramatic focus for the next two decades. *Miss Saigon,* written by Alain Boublil and Claude-Michel Schönberg, the creators of *Les Misérables,* and produced by Cameron Mackintosh, was a bona fide hit when it opened at the Theatre Royal, Drury Lane, in London in 1989. With its success, both critical and commercial, the decision to transfer the play to Broadway was easy. However, its movement to the Great White Way did not go smoothly in the summer of 1990. Jonathan Pryce, a Welsh actor, originated the role of The Engineer, a Eurasian pimp, playing the role with taped eye lids to give him a more pronounced Asian appearance. Mackintosh intended for Pryce to continue the role in the Broadway production, but the Asian American theater community, which had seen its theatrical power rise with the success of *M. Butterfly,* struck back at Mackintosh's casting, citing Price's yellow-face portrayal as culturally offensive. After all, if blackface is unacceptable, then why should yellowface be tolerated in the 1990s? Questions were also raised as to why Mackintosh was not seeking an Asian performer for the Broadway production. B. D. Wong and Hwang both wrote letters to Actor's Equity complaining about the casting of a Caucasian man in an Asian role, especially since numerous talented Asian American actors were not working as a result of the limited availability of Asian roles and the reluctance of casting directors to cast against race. With a plum role finally available, why were they not being auditioned? Actor's Equity debated the points raised by Wong, Hwang, and others and voted in their favor, denying Pryce the role on Broadway, even though the production had already sold $24 million in advance tickets.

Furious over the decision, Mackintosh, seeing the union's decision as an infringement on his and Pryce's artistic autonomy as well as a promotion of censorship, canceled the production, effectively ending its move to Broadway. Actor's Equity's decision and Mackintosh's response provoked a two-week media uproar that crossed international borders as the media and artists debated the merits of ethnic representation in the theater versus freedom of expression and artistic choices made by the artistic members of a production.[1] Capturing the political tenor of the early 1990s, the issue was framed as an example of censorship caused by affirmative action. Muddying the controversy was the character description of The Engineer as half-French and half-Vietnamese, thus allowing the casting of an actor from a much wider pool of ethnic types than strictly Asian. Under pressure from Mackintosh's cancellation of the production, which would cause more than thirty performers of Asian, African, and Hispanic American heritage to lose their roles in the cast as well as the disappearance of $24 million in ticket purchases, Actor's Equity reversed its decision.[2] Hwang, Wong, and the others lost their protest over the casting, although Mackintosh announced that he would cast an Asian as The Engineer after Pryce finished his run. Hwang's reaction to the event was notable disappointment. "Unfortunately, we never had the public discussion the situation merited. There was an economic agenda to get that show on Broadway, and the issue we raised never got a full airing."[3] As a debater might, he could see both arguments, acknowledging that "I felt for both sides," but he qualified this recognition by suggesting that "I don't think they would have reacted the same way if it had been a Japanese producer bringing in a Japanese actor to play an American."[4] However, the long-term result of the protest was clear in Hwang's mind, as "in the future no one will cast a white actor in a major Asian role without at least thinking twice about it."[5] Despite the raised attention to the dearth of Asian roles, Asian performers still faced an uphill battle in finding roles: as Hwang noted, "the fact remains that 90 percent of the stage productions in this country still employ all-white casts, and in any other industry we'd have to say that's a pretty rotten minority hiring record. That question needs to be addressed because Caucasians are increasingly becoming a plurality rather than a majority in this country, and you don't want to get into a sort of artistic apartheid situation where a minority of people control a majority of the artistic resources simply on the basis of some self-defined aesthetic superiority."[6]

When *Yellow Face* was performed in Chicago in the summer of 2011, interviewers asked Hwang for his impression of the *Miss Saigon* controversy twenty years after the fact. He noted that there were two elements that drove the controversy: employment and aesthetics. In terms of hiring he noted that "we are still not at a point where we would cast James Earl Jones as George Washington and as long as that is the case and race still matters in theater, if we don't cast minorities in minority roles, than [*sic*] what parts are they going to play?"[7] When it came to aesthetics, he used the example of Brian Friel's *Dancing at Lughnasa,* which premiered on Broadway with an all-Irish cast. Once the cast finished its run, the actors were replaced by Americans. Hwang observed: "Some people think that the Irish cast was better. So, if that's the case, it is sometimes true that if you cast actors that have more experience in the stories that they're portraying, and whose own experience is closer to the experience that they are portraying, maybe you're going to get a better production. But I can also see where there are aesthetic reasons why there are interesting reasons to go against that sometimes, too."[8] However, in the long run, Hwang's perspective came down to artistic freedom, which, in his mind, takes precedence. "Producers and writers have the right to cast whoever they want. But I also believe that people who don't like their decisions have the right to complain as loudly as they want as well."[9] While Hwang would not publicly protest the decision over the ensuing years, he would use the controversy as a catalyst for his writing, as he began to explore the complicated nature of ethnic identity and membership as the country approached the start of a new millennium.

Bondage

Bondage was Hwang's first foray back into the theater after the controversy surrounding *Miss Saigon.* In having his newest play open at the Humana Festival, an annual festival for new writing held in Louisville, Kentucky, "a nice, low-pressure environment," where the play would be judged on its own merits rather than in light of his recent rabble-rousing notoriety, he aimed to avoid the publicity that his name would generate by having the premiere in a larger venue.[10] The play premiered on March 1, 1992.

During the decade after his graduation from Stanford, Hwang changed his opinion about ethnicity. He no longer subscribed to his collegiate isolationist/ nationalistic perspective. Instead, he now believed that skin color should not be the predominant defining nature of an individual. In fact, Hwang decided that one's skin color "doesn't tell us anything useful about the individual,"[11] and in *Bondage* he set out to prove that point. In order to explore the concept of ethnicity without the characters' ethnicities getting in the way, Hwang had both actors covered entirely from head to toe in bondage gear, hiding the ethnicity of the actor and character, thus allowing all sorts of permutations to occur in the casting. (The cast in Louisville was composed of B. D. Wong, an Asian male, and Kathryn Layng, a Caucasian female, and the script reflects that fact.) In so doing, he created a truly blind experience for the audience in terms of ethnic connections and prejudices. He explained that his choice of costume "allows us to begin playing with this notion of the interchangeability of skin colors and how they do or do not relate to particular behavior."[12] Jon Rossini complimented Hwang's savvy decision to use an S&M parlor as the play's setting because the space aids in reinforcing his exploration of ethnic relationships. Rossini wrote that "it seems clear that we are in a space in which a personal fantasy becomes reflective of larger societal concerns, and a model of sexual relations becomes a template for dissecting different forms of human relationships."[13] Also driving Hwang's focus in the play was an autobiographical connection. He had divorced Ophelia in 1989 and a few years later began dating his future wife, Kathryn Layng, one of the co-stars of *Bondage.* Hwang's first marriage was to a Chinese Canadian woman, but his relationship with Layng placed him in an interracial relationship, which opened up new questions and concerns about stereotypes and expectations embedded in each of their identity classes—blonde, Caucasian woman for Layng and Chinese American, violin-playing man for Hwang. As a couple, they had to navigate their own preconceptions of racial identity as well as the societal stereotypes embedded in their racial designations. Layng admitted that their relationship found its way into the words of the characters: "*Bondage* was a deeply personal work. . . . I saw David in it so much, myself in it, the discussions, the breaking through of stereotypes when you're with someone who is the Other. It was really a priceless experience for us as a couple."[14]

The play takes place in a southern California S&M parlor during a session between Terri, a dominatrix, and Mark, her submissive. It opens as they engage in a role-playing game of ethnic types; she declares herself a blonde woman and tells him he is a Chinese man. In their regular sessions, Terri manipulates Mark into declaring "I love you" to the various ethnic female types she enacts. When he professes his love, he has submitted to the unobtainable fantasy woman and has placed himself at the lowest level of humiliation. On this day, though, Terri is struggling to maintain her professional demeanor, allowing her tough ethnic feminine facades to slip, while Mark has a desire not to play the role of his usual submissive self. The interchange between the two characters moves between their real-life personas and the various ethnic scenarios that Terri crafts, including African American woman/Caucasian man, Asian American woman/Asian American man, and Caucasian woman/Caucasian man. In each one of the scenarios Terri manages to better Mark by trapping him into an unflattering, stereotypical performance of a particular ethnicity. However, the game for Terri no longer offers her any fulfillment. She has grown tired of the role playing and wants to engage with Mark one on one as their true, undisguised selves. At the play's end she strips off all of her bondage gear except for her mask, which she demands that Mark remove. He, though, refuses to do so and strips off his own mask, revealing that he is an Asian male, while she takes her own mask off and reveals that she is a blonde, Caucasian woman, the role-playing identities that began the play. The two resolve to explore their relationship out in the open in the eyes of society, instead of within the confined and private fantasy space of the S&M parlor.

Like *M. Butterfly*, *Bondage* offers a relationship that relies upon fantasy in order to exist. However, in contrast to Gallimard's twenty-year-long fantasy of believing that Song is a woman, Mark's fantasies occur during an hourly session, and the fantastical relationships are created at his own urging. While Terri decides what role-playing fantasy game they will enact at each meeting, he willingly and actively participates, making comments and critiquing the nature of the fantasy Terri has created. Even though Mark is powerless in the games with Terri, he is powerful in that he chooses to be the submissive member. Gallimard, though, realizes that he has been at the whim of Song's manipulation and at this point acknowledges the fantasy of his relationship, choosing to become Butterfly. Jon Rossini discussed the different use of fantasy in the two pieces, noting that "in *Bondage*, Hwang has his character Mark, specifically a Chinese American man, choose to play through the fantasy in order to expose cultural modes of construction and, ideally, explode them. This process is in direct opposition to the close of *M. Butterfly*, in which Gallimard, the European man, was given the opportunity to 'choose fantasy.'"[15]

As in *Sound and Beauty* and *M. Butterfly*, Hwang presents the antagonism that exists between males and females, highlighting again their suspicion and distrust of each other. However, the difference in *Bondage* is that he captures the additional level of antagonism that exists when race and individual prejudices are added into the relationship equation. The opening salvo between a blonde woman and an Asian man introduces this recurring dynamic. With their roles assigned by Terri, Mark begins the fantasy sequence by approaching Terri, who has already pigeonholed Mark's Asian identity. For Terri, the man before her embodies the nerdy, brainy, science-oriented stereotype. She tells him: "I've seen you looking at me. From behind the windows of your—engineering laboratory. Behind your—horn-rimmed glasses. Why don't you come right out and try to pick me up? Whisper something offensive into my ear. Or aren't you man enough?"[16] She attributes to him the characteristics of the shy Asian man, cowed by blonde beauties, too enamored of his work and afraid of women outside his own race. Mark reinforces this type by admitting his uncertainty in approaching her: "But—you're a blonde. I'm—Chinese. It's not so easy to know whether it's OK for me to love you" (253). She regales him about the new time period in which they live, telling him: "C'mon, this is the 1990s! I'm no figment of the past. For a Chinese man to love a white woman—what could be wrong about that?" (254). However, as soon as she draws him in with these words of encouragement, she dismantles him with more ethnic stereotyping, admitting: "I would never be prejudiced against an Oriental. They have such . . . strong family structures . . . hard-working . . . they hit the books with real gusto . . . makes my mother green with envy. But, I guess . . . how excited can I get about a boy who fulfills my mother's fantasies?" (254). Asian males, therefore, will always be a safe, respectable choice, but she has no interest in safety. She craves danger, some-one "I can regret in later life" (254), and Asian males are not threatening at all, just as Song intimates in *M. Butterfly,* when he says he can never be considered a man because he is Asian. Terri even admits that she chooses the Asian male role for Mark when she is having an off day precisely because of the lack of masculine traits associated with that ethnic group.

Just as she does in the Caucasian-woman/Asian-man scenario, in the rest of their pairings Terri easily parries all Mark's attempts to gain the upper hand and pigeonholes him in a stereotypical role by turning his words against him. For example, when she announces that they will now become an Asian woman and an Asian male, she emasculates him by relaying Asian women's desire to go out with white men instead of their ethnic brothers. She tells him that "Asian men have oppressed their women for centuries. Now, they're paying for their crimes by being passed over for dates in favor of white men. It's a beautiful way to look at history, when you think about it" (268). In each role-playing game, she frames the men as oppressive not only toward their ethnic female partner but also toward women in general. In doing so, she reinforces the Hwangian theme of distrustful and antagonistic relations between men and women.

Through all the enacted scenarios the two characters are completely covered in leather, allowing Hwang to depict the fluidity of identity. Both characters, lacking physical ethnic descriptors, move effortlessly among the various roles that they enact, especially Terri, whose profession requires that she research all the permutations of racial couplings, so she is prepared for her client. As Terri says near the end of the play, "I've been a man. I've been a woman. I've been colorful and colorless" (277). When Mark pledges to defeat her in one of their exchanges, she crows back, "This is your game—to play all the races—but me—I've already become all races. You came to the wrong place, sucker. Inside this costume live the intimate experiences of ethnic groups that haven't even been born" (265). The audience, not knowing the ethnicity of the actors, must accept at face value the words said by the characters in their various roles (after all, Terri may actually be an Asian or an African American woman under all that leather) and engage with the ideas being expressed about the biases and stereotypes of that specific ethnic group. The leather masks therefore allow the audience to project onto the actor's covered face the ethnic character being portrayed. In so doing, not only does Terri but both actors become all races, enabled by the audience's willing participation in the creation of those ethnic roles. Mark and Terri and the actors playing them become Everyman and Everywoman.

However, there is still the question of why Mark needs such an experience at Terri's hands. What does he gain through the various antagonistic ethnic pairings? In the real world Mark finds himself trapped, as the stereotypes associated with his skin color have kept him oppressed. His confusion and the ensuing disempowerment in his various relationships are palpable. Because of his ethnicity, he is born to lose. Such identity predeterminations by others are something Hwang and Asian Americans experience daily. Hwang has recounted in numerous interviews the fact that when a non-Asian sees an Asian on the street, the non-Asian assumes that the Asian person comes from another country, even though the Asian person may have been born in the United States. Hwang said: "It's almost as if one's features give off the wrong information. It's the way people choose to process that information that misleads them, and we often pay the price for it one way or another."[17] With such notions about ethnicity so prevalent, how can one have a sense of self-identity if that identity has already been predetermined by society? By escaping into the S&M parlor Mark acquires safety and surety from such preconceptions and judgments. The anonymity of his mask protects him from all of Terri's pigeonholing. He explains to her that "The rules here . . . protect me from harm. Out there—I walk around with my face exposed. In here, when I'm rejected, beaten down, humiliated—it's not me" (271). There is, in other words, a comfort to be found in these fictionalized rejections precisely because they are not real and not based on his true ethnic identity and self. In addition, while he can lose his battles with Terri, he loses because of the rules of a game he created rather than rules created by societal stereotypes and prejudices.

At the end of the play both reveal their true identities—Terri is a blonde Caucasian woman, Mark is a Chinese American male—and decide to give their relationship a chance outside the walls of the bondage parlor and within the fabric of the prejudiced American society. Mark expresses concern about what they may find: "I worry when I think about the coming millennium. Because it feels like all labels have to be rewritten, all assumptions reexamined, all associations redefined. The rules that governed behavior in the last era are crumbling, but those of the time to come have yet to be written. And there is a struggle brewing over the shape of these changing words, a struggle that begins here, now, in our hearts, in our shuttered rooms, in the lightning decisions that appear from nowhere" (277). Mark's words and the mixed racial pairing of the couple at the end of Hwang's play is prescient in terms of what would occur over the coming decades in the United States as mixed racial relations become more accepted and, even, in some cases, taken for granted. After all, an entire generation of American youth has been raised to accept mixed racial relationships as the norm and do not see any problems with interracial romance. However, for Mark and Terri in the early 1990s, during the height of political correctness and amid the culture wars that dominated the United States political and social scene, the comforting future is still far away, and they will encounter travails, but rather than confronting the stereotypes in an antagonistic nature, as they did in the bondage parlor, they will now be linked as a couple, fighting together against prejudices and preconceptions of race.

Face Value

After writing the one-act *Bondage,* with its focused look on the complexity of racial identity, Hwang approached the topic in a much larger, broader framework with an eye toward Broadway, turning racial misidentification into comedy in the full-length play *Face Value.* In 1989 Hwang began mulling over writing a farce that would use mistaken racial identity as its comic through line. However, "I couldn't really think of a plot line. I couldn't really think why anyone would disguise himself as a member of another race. When *Saigon* came along, here was an instance where someone actually was doing that."[18] Literary inspirations included Joe Orton's farces *Loot* and *What the Butler Saw,* which not only featured slamming doors, mistaken identities, and hanky-panky but also provided biting criticism of English society and government institutions in the 1960s. Hwang saw the current controversies surrounding race as fitting perfectly within an Ortonesque model. Hwang explained that in *Face Value* "everyone ends up having to be in a different race than their own by the end. It really speaks to the randomness of race—theoretically, anyone can wind up behind any face."[19] Another influence was Luigi Pirandello's *Six Characters in Search of an Author,* which features a metatheatrical dissection of the line between actors and characters. At the start of the second act of *Face Value* Linda steps out of character and addresses the audience: "Ladies and gentlemen I just can't go on with this play. I've been feeling for some time now . . . this is such a negative portrayal of an Asian woman."[20] All the other actors are thereby prompted to critique their own roles' ethnic depictions. Partly driving the work was Hwang's movement away from the tenets of multiculturalism. "I prefer the term I made up, interculturalism. I think it's more important to use our different identities to teach each other, to learn from each other. Why limit ourselves to say I only take experiences from my tribe?"[21]

Face Value takes place on opening night of a bad musical about Fu Manchu, which features song lyrics like "Cruel yet transcendental / He's a crafty oriental."[22] Similar to the *Miss Saigon*'s casting kerfuffle, the actor playing Fu Manchu, Bernie Sugarman, is not Asian but Jewish, playing the role in yellowface. An Asian actress, Linda Ann Wing, upset with the casting, convinces her Asian male friend Randall Lee, who is secretly in love with her, to disrupt the opening night by sneaking into the theater in whiteface so that they can mingle seamlessly with the white audience and then denounce the production midshow. In addition, two white supremacists, having infiltrated the theater, plan on kidnapping Sugarman, believing that he is Asian. Hwang rounds out the cast with an African American female stage manager, Marci, who speaks flawless Chinese; a stereotypical dumb-blonde chorus girl, Jessica, who has been having a fling with Sugarman but later finds herself attracted to the whitefaced Randall; and Andrew, the play's harried producer, who ends up falling for Marci, realizing during a blackout that they have more in common than he thought. After the play is disrupted by the protest, the supremacists hold Bernie and Linda hostage. In an effort to rescue Sugarman, many of the characters dress up as Fu Manchu to confuse the supremacists. In the end almost all the characters end up wearing a different racial mask from their own, resulting in ethnic confusion but also multiracial romantic pairings.

Face Value was scheduled for an out-of-town tryout in Boston in February 1993 before opening on Broadway. However, the reviews from newspaper critics found a number of problems with Hwang's farcical take on the *Miss Saigon* controversy. The *Christian Science Monitor*'s April Austin had little positive to say, noting that the plot was so convoluted that she "got lost trying to explain it to a colleague." It featured "pointless wackiness," suggesting that "farce isn't his forte." More important, his desire to theatricalize the racial issues created a play that "fails to register as either comedy or protest" because "it skims across important issues without once dipping below the surface." Iris Fanger of the *Boston Herald* was equally dismissive, describing the experience of watching the play as "squirmy viewing." Hwang's writing was problematic, with its "zingy one-liners that Hwang throws off as if he's the next Neil Simon" and "preachy lessons." Most troublesome was the play's structure. As Fanger noted, "The climax comes at the first act curtain, leaving the second act to meander in search of a reason to keep the audience in its seats." Kevin Kelly of the *Boston Globe* compared *Face Value* to a sketch one might see on *Saturday Night Live*. The farcical nature of the play worked against the racial questions and concerns Hwang was trying to raise. Kelly appreciated Hwang's attempt to respond to the controversy, but the "hammering articulation is as trying as vaudeville," and instead of raising the discussion about race, the play "stumbles down to Hallmark platitudes." At the end of the review Kelly asks: "Is *Face Value* salvageable?" His answer? "On the face of it, it doesn't seem so. To employ its own backhanded humor, too much stir-fry in the farce."[23]

Despite the scathing reviews, Hwang believed that he could make the necessary fixes before the play's Broadway opening. Once the play began previews in Manhattan it quickly became apparent that the work was not ready to premiere, and the producers shut the production down after only eight previews at a cost of $2 million. Afterwards, Hwang was sanguine about the play's failure, noting "I suspect that the audience just didn't believe in the characters. The farce wasn't grounded enough in psychological reality."[24] In addition, he found fault with his decision making in the creative process, acknowledging the difficulty of writing farce. He surmised that it might have been better if he had done the play as a social satire, like a Molière play. As with *Rich Relations,* Hwang still drew a positive result from the experience in terms of his writing. Because of the international success of *M. Butterfly,* Hwang had felt incredible pressure to make sure that his next play was even better than *M. Butterfly.* "Once you have a hit the size of *M. Butterfly,* there's always a demon that lives in your mind saying, 'Am I doing as well? Can I do the same or top this?' That demon has nothing to do with the aesthetic process, and is probably injurious to it. But I think it's pretty hard to avoid."[25] By producing a well-publicized commercial flop, he removed any kind of pressure for his future productions. Instead, he could "go back to being a regular playwright."[26]

Face Value has not been revived. However, Hwang never allowed the larger motif of ethnicity and the truth of cultural identity to drift far from his mind. Over the ensuing years he would return to the topic in various short plays, but it would be fifteen years before he would finally write *Yellow Face*, which successfully accomplished what he was trying to do in *Face Value*. Before writing that Obie Award–winning play, he had a personal story about his family to convey.

Golden Child

With his first full-length play since *Face Value*, Hwang returned to dramatizing his family, but, unlike *Rich Relations* and *Family Devotions*, which were based on his immediate and extended family members, *Golden Child* looks back into his family's history when his mother's side of the family converted to Christianity. Interestingly, the source material derives from a piece of juvenilia written by Hwang when he was ten years old. Hearing that his maternal grandmother in the Philippines was ill, he asked his parents for permission to travel from California to Cebu in the Philippines to spend the summer with her. Reflecting on that impetuous decision to leave his family and travel over the Pacific, reversing the route taken by his parents twenty years earlier, he mused: "It is sort of striking, really, that I thought it was important to know what my family history was, and that I went to see her that summer and we did these oral histories. In retrospect I think it has to do with needing to understand myself in the context of being a Chinese-American growing up in Southern California, when there were a lot fewer Asians than there are now."[27] While in the Philippines, he recorded his grandmother's stories and then, when he returned home, transcribed them into a novella called *Only Three Generations*. The title was inspired by the Chinese proverb "The wealth of a Chinese family lasts only three generations."[28]

In contrast to his cynical depiction of religion in his earlier family dramas, he was intent on being evenhanded in addressing his ancestors' conversion to Christianity, admitting that "I must interpret the past without falling into either demonizing or unquestioning acceptance."[29] While the play addresses the period of conversion, Hwang admits that the relationship between his family and the type of religion they practice now is much more complicated, as it is not exclusively Christian. At extended family gatherings at Christmas, his grandmother would tell "a story about a relative who was kidnapped by pirates and sold to a Chinese-Christian family, who brought him up to be dedicated to God. The message was that since he was dedicated to God, we as his descendants should be, too. The story was actually old-fashioned

Chinese ancestor worship dressed up in Christian drag—but since stories like this were delivered to me as a child under the heading of Christian ideology, it was hard to pick out what was actually Chinese."[30] Their worship instead might be described as an amalgamation of Christian and Chinese practices. While his contemporary family's religious situation is far more complicated in its blending of Christian and Chinese values, the story of the conversion of his ancestors is far more straightforward, and the play accurately depicts this critical moment in his family's history. "As in the play, my great-grandfather did convert to Christianity, at which point he unbound his daughter's feet. The first and third of his wives died, and he was left with the one who was the most ambitious. My grandmother's mother, his first wife, died of opium addiction. And my grandmother is, to this day, very fundamentalist Christian in her religious beliefs."[31]

While Hwang had previously expanded the ethnic scope of the American family play with *Family Devotions, Golden Child* entered new territory, especially by focusing on the three wives of the household. Hwang hoped his story about a Chinese family in the early part of the twentieth century would connect with an audience more accustomed to traditional American family dramas. He commented: "Using this different setup as a sort of prism, I hope audiences can see topics that family plays have dealt with for centuries, but through new eyes."[32] In addition to placing his work within the canon of family dramas, he also thought of *Golden Child* as a memory play like Tennessee Williams's *The Glass Menagerie* and Brian Friel's *Dancing at Lughnasa,* both of which feature a modern-day narrator. In Hwang's play, though, the more he reworked the story, the more his narrator became an increasingly diminishing component. In addition, Hwang set himself "the challenge of trying to move an audience just with my words."[33] In order to accomplish that task, Hwang looked further back in dramatic history for inspiration, settling on one of the masters of the modern era, Anton Chekhov, who, through his words in *The Three Sisters* and *The Cherry Orchard,* captured the details of the smaller, quieter moments of life, while eschewing the gigantic dramatic moments on which most playwrights relied for emotional impact. Hwang joked with interviewers that instead of writing *The Three Sisters,* he had written *The Three Wives.* It is worth mentioning that Hwang's plays, to this point, had been dominated by male characters, and *M. Butterfly* received criticism for its stereotypical depiction of its Eastern and Western female characters. So it is notable to recognize Hwang's decision to focus the play around four female characters, three wives and one daughter. One might surmise that *Golden Child* was Hwang's reply to some of his *M. Butterfly* critics.

Golden Child premiered ten years after *M. Butterfly*, on April 2, 1998 at the Longacre Theatre. Unlike the short production time accorded *M. Butterfly* (and even the unsuccessful *Face Value*) between its out-of-town tryout and its move to Broadway, *Golden Child* took an incredibly circuitous route to the Great White Way. Originally commissioned by South Coast Repertory Company in Costa Mesa, California, *Golden Child*, which Hwang began writing in 1995, had a peripatetic career in a variety of locations, including the Public Theater in New York, the Kennedy Center in Washington, D. C., the American Conservatory Theatre in San Francisco, and the Singapore Repertory Theatre, before opening on Broadway. In between the various productions, Hwang tweaked the play to address issues discovered during the previous performances. One of the main problems he initially faced was how to determine the proper balance between the contemporary story and the one from the past. At first the contemporary story dominated the work, with his contemporary characters using monologues to talk about the family's ancestral figures. As the play went through its various productions, the contemporary story and its monologues were increasingly stripped away, while the story from the past was developed further, allowing the historical characters to have their own voices. Eventually, the contemporary story was converted into a framing device for the past.

James Lapine directed this latter version of *Golden Child* as an off-Broadway production at the Public Theater, and it opened on November 17, 1996. Ben Brantley, writing for the *New York Times*, described *Golden Child* as "this earnest, sweet-tempered work by a dramatist who is teaching himself to look back not in anger but forgiveness." Brantley noted the familiar religious material of *Family Devotions* but commented that, in contrast to the earlier play, Hwang now displayed "the evenhandedness of a debate moderator" as his play "maintains an air of instructional temperance" and has moments of being "very poignant." Despite the words of praise, ultimately Brantley decided that the play did not succeed because of a lack of dramatic urgency and observed that the memory narrative device created a "light anesthetic" for the audience. Essentially, the play failed to be "emotionally gripping." John Lahr of *The New Yorker* offered a positive response, seeing a much larger issue of audience awareness at stake in the work. He argued that *Golden Child* "opens up the parochial heart of the audience to a sense of otherness—not just the otherness of the Asian community but the strangeness of all of us who consider ourselves 'American.'"[34]

After the play's run at the Public, there was an initial desire to transfer the production to Broadway, but eventually the producers agreed that it still needed more work, including the bookended nature of the contemporary character and his story. Hwang returned to his source material for inspiration, where he "came upon a scene involving my great-grandfather's decision to unbind my grandmother's feet, reversing a centuries-old tradition which had turned women into cripples in the name of feminine beauty. Such a moment had only been talked about but not dramatized in the Public production."[35] With this new element in place, the play moved to the Kennedy Center, but Hwang had dialed up the humor far too much in the new incarnation, thus erasing the emotional impact of the play's ending. Once again, a planned Broadway transfer was delayed. The play then traveled to Singapore for a run at the Singapore Repertory Company. Hwang once again made alterations, making the lead male character older, thus adding more gravitas to his decision to convert to Christianity. The disruption to his family was now not the action of a rash young man but instead the rationalized decision of an experienced older man. The play's run in Singapore resulted in a personal connection between Hwang and his audience. "As the child of immigrants, I felt a particular pride in the response of the Singaporean Chinese, many of whom told me that the work had caused them to rediscover their own ancestral histories."[36] For the American Conservatory Theatre production in San Francisco Hwang added more motivation for the husband's decision to convert and developed the individualized relationships he had with his three wives. At that point, all involved decided the play was Broadway bound.

At the play's Broadway debut, *Variety*'s Matt Wolf noted the same problem mentioned by Brantley two years earlier, namely the absence of dramatic action. He wrote: "The burden of ancestry may be one of many provocative concerns in David Henry Hwang's *Golden Child*, but such issues ultimately pale next to a more immediate obligation—to be dramatic—that the play just does not meet." He praised the presence of intriguing thematic and theatrical elements but cited Hwang for failing to do them justice. "The play is as staid as it is self-evidently sincere, and all its alternately and melodramatic passages merely amplify Hwang's failure to bring some fascinating themes to urgent, needful life." Peter Marks, writing for the *New York Times,* echoed the same issue as his colleagues—the lack of dramatic urgency. Marks compared the vibrant theatricality of *M. Butterfly* with the lack of such theatricality in *Golden Child*, observing that Hwang "hasn't figured out how to infuse a less sensational tale with the narrative force and energy necessary to animate a Broadway stage." Instead, he called the work more "of a boiled-down novel than a theater piece." And, in a final stab at Hwang's play, Marks compared it to "one of those ponderous costume dramas that *Masterpiece Theater* has resorted to showing."[37] Despite the criticism, the play received three Tony Award nominations, including one for best play. However, the play's time on Broadway was short-lived, lasting only for sixty-nine performances.

The final version of the play features a truncated contemporary book-ended story of Andrew, a writer, unable to sleep as he worries about the impending birth of his first child. As he lies awake, he is visited by Ahn, his dead grandmother, who reminds him of her story of growing up at a time of great change in her family. The scene transforms back to a village near Amoy in 1918 as Ahn anticipates the return of Tieng-Bin, her father, home from the Philippines after having been gone for three years. Tieng-Bin has three wives: Siu-Yong, his first wife, the most traditional and Ahn's mother; Luan, the most practical but Tieng-Bin's least favorite; and Eling, his youngest and most attractive wife. The three women live in an uneasy alliance based on suspicion as they run the household together. They too look forward to Tieng-Bin's return but with some trepidation, unsure of how much he has been influenced by his time away from China. Luan, though, sees an opportunity to gain control of the household, if Tieng-Bin decides to challenge the established ways of their country. When he returns, he begins to praise Western marvels and criticizes Chinese ways, such as the binding of a woman's feet, and at the end of the first act he has Ahn's feet unbound. In the second act Baines, a missionary, begins to visit Tieng-Bin, trying to convert him to Christianity. After much concern about the effect on his ancestors, Tieng-Bin is convinced by Baines's arguments to convert his entire household. The dilemma for the wives is concern over the possible fallout from such a decision, since Tieng-Bin can have only one Christian wife. Siu-Yong, who becomes more and more addicted to opium to deal with the Western changes in the household, commits suicide rather than convert. Eling dies in childbirth, prompted to die by Siu-Yong's ghost, leaving Tieng-Bin with his one Christian wife, Luan, his least favorite. Despite the death of Siu-Yong, Ahn's future is guaranteed to be different from her mother's. The future for her now has far more possibilities, and, with her story told, Andrew feels more secure about the future for his child.

Rather than explore his previous interest in the struggles between men and women, Hwang focuses the first portion of the play on the domestic and marital competition among Tieng-Bin's three wives. Even though each woman has her identity defined by her hierarchical position, each is unhappy with her assigned roles. The animosity among them is highlighted early, as Hwang conveys their competition through the wives' apparent display of respect to one another, even though their comments contain quite the bite.

ELING: Dearest Elder Sister, forgive me for my disrespect. I know I will
    never be able to match the great wisdom you have gained from having
    lived so many more years on this earth than me.
LUAN: Thank you, Little Sister. Forgive *me*. When husband made you his
    concubine, I took a solemn vow never to remind you of your peasant
    birth, or the fact that you were originally brought here to be my servant.
    I only pray that one day you will manage to bear him a child.[38]

During Tieng-Bin's absence, the wives worry about changes that might occur
upon his return. Siu-Yong does not want any type of change to happen so
that she might maintain her status and position, plus her freedom to smoke
opium. Without any changes, the household stays for Siu-Yong a place of
comfort, safety, and reliability. For her, the wives' roles are imbedded in
the ritualized nature of a woman's place in Chinese society, and any change
brings disgrace and the losing of face to the family. She instructs Ahn about
her feminine duty in her future husband's household: "To preserve the family
is your first duty as a woman. If you fail, your children and grandchildren
will abandon you in your old age; and when you die, your face will fade
slowly from their memories, and your name will be forgotten" (26). Luan,
in contrast, covets only power, and Siu-Yong's seniority and Eling's youth are
hurdles to her claiming control of the household. As the second wife, she is
imprisoned by her status as secondary to the respected position of the first
wife, and she has no sway with Tieng-Bin because the third wife's beauty
captivates him. The only way she can attain power is through the manipulation of her fellow wives and, more important, her husband. For Eling, given
her young age and her inexperience in the battles among the wives, she just
wants to be loved exclusively by her husband. With his attentions upon her,
she does not have to worry about the household struggles for dominance.

    With Tieng-Bin's return, the wives' suspicions about his being influenced
by the West are confirmed, signaling that disruptions to their lives are immi-
nent. These begin at dinner, when Tieng-Bin bestows a gift upon each wife.
To Siu-Yong, he gives a cuckoo clock. Her dismayed reaction is apparent
from her response: "I'm sure it will do wonders for my insomnia" (18). To
Luan, he gives a waffle iron. Shocked, she remarks that "it's so beautiful, I
can hardly imagine actually using it" (18). To Eling, he gives a phonograph,
and she admits that "It's so . . . primitive, so crude and barbaric. I like it!"
(18). While the gifts represent the introduction of Western influences into
the house, each one also reinforces Tieng-Bin's view of each wife and his
relationship with her. The clock represents Siu-Yong as the representative of

order and domestic control over the house, reifying her superiority over the other wives but also implying that her domestic position revolves around her role as head of the household rather than as his wife. Luan's gift is for the kitchen, a domestic item to aid in her making food for him; he views her, like Siu-Yong, as a domestic who will serve and cook for him. Eling's gift, though, is distinctly different. The phonograph is an extravagance. The clock and the waffle maker can be viewed as necessary instruments in the daily workings of an early twentieth-century home, but a phonograph is not a household necessity ensuring the smooth running of the house. Tieng-Bin's gift is intended as a luxury item and is a private gift for the two of them to enjoy in Eling's bedroom, indicating that, while the other two wives are expected to work, his third wife is simply expected to enjoy.

Ahn considers her father's arrival with Western gifts as an opportunity to push for further changes in her own life. At dinner, as her father talks of backward Eastern practices, she asks:

AHN: Would that mean I could take the bindings off my feet?
SIU-YONG: Ahn!
AHN: My feet hurt so bad at night—and they stink, too! (13)

By the end of the first act, Tieng-Bin decides to forgo tradition and have her feet unwrapped. His dramatic action announces that the established system, which injures women, is not to be tolerated in his household. He asks: "Why should we cling to a tradition that only passes down suffering from one generation to the next?" (28). Much like the characters in *Bondage* who recognize a changing future that will become more open to mixed-race couples, Tieng-Bin foresees the possibilities opening up for women in the immediate future. He tells his wives: "The world is changing. There's a whole new generation of men who will want an educated wife. Not some backwards girl hobbling around on rotting feet, filling the room with the stench of death!" (13). His wives are shocked by his pronouncement, but Luan later, in a bid to gain favor with him, supports his decision, telling him: "As for myself, the idea of having a daughter—with beautiful, gigantic feet—it excites me" (27). However, Tieng-Bin's decision does not come easily. To unbind his daughter's feet is to run counter to the actions of generations of family members who came before him. To break with such a tradition is to dishonor his ancestors. Tieng-Bin struggles with the consequences of such an action: "Oh, I can hear you—and all the ancestors—crying from beyond, 'Some things cannot be changed.' But don't I have the right to try? I accept all responsibility, assume all consequences" (28).

While the unbinding of Ahn's feet goes against tradition, displeasing his ancestors, his flirtation with Christianity poses a much larger threat. The unbinding of Ahn's feet affects one individual in the household, but his choice to pursue Christianity will disrupt the entire household.

LUAN: If Husband becomes a Christian, then everything changes. All roles around here are up for reassignment. And the one who breaks the most rules wins.

SIU-YONG: Foreigners have been invading our country for centuries. We always change them more than they change us. It won't be any different this time. (20)

Of the three wives, Luan understands best the consequence if he converts. Siu-Yong refuses to see the threat, believing that once again East will best West. However, Siu-Yong also knows that if such a change were to occur, then Luan could unseat her. She warns her: "Stay away from the preacher. If you try to show me up by becoming a Christian, I'll see to it that you're demoted to a common concubine" (21). Not trusting Luan, Siu-Yong sends Ahn to the meetings with the minister to keep an eye on the second wife, which results in Ahn's desire to convert to Christianity. Through the scheming of her mother, Ahn succumbs to the temptations of the West. In contrast to the other wives, Eling enjoys the Western objects that her husband brings her, although she uses them only in the privacy of her bedroom. She lounges in the Western lingerie he has bought especially for her and finds the opera music of the West enticing. She tells her husband: "I like this *Traviata*. It fills me with feelings. Modern feelings. Delicious feelings of . . . power" (23). Her openness to Western influences, however, extends only to the pleasures they bestow. When faced with adopting the West's religious beliefs, she is reluctant to abandon her worship of her ancestors. For her, such a change goes too far. Hwang explained the importance of ancestor worship: "Ancestor worship isn't religion per se, but simply an extension of a Confucian belief system. Essentially, you don't ever really grow up. Even when your parents die, you have a subservient relationship with them because you fear that if you don't do this or that, their ghosts are going to come get you. It's pragmatic."[39] The play highlights the ancestor worship of the family, showing each character at different times saying prayers to his or her family members before altars set up in the character's rooms.

Tieng-Bin's choice to become Christian is not an easy one. He too, like Eling, is torn between his obligation to his ancestors and the temptation of the Western religion. After all, his entire identity has been framed through his relationship to his ancestors. Everything he has done and become is to aid them in the next world. The weight of the past lies heavy upon Tieng-Bin, more than on any of Hwang's other characters who have faced the temptation to choose the West over the East. He understands the importance of such a decision in disrupting his own identity: "But to be Chinese—means to feel a whole web of obligation—obligation?—dating back 5,000 years. I am afraid of dishonoring my ancestors, even the ones dead for centuries. All the time, I feel the ghosts—sitting on my back, whispering in my ear—keeping me from living life as I see fit" (33–34). Partly driving Tieng-Bin's possible willingness to overthrow five thousand years of history is the fact that he is beginning to view himself through a Western lens. He has known the sense of being defined only through his ancestors, as the weight of the past is on his shoulders as his actions in the present influence the larger ancestral line of family pride and face. The missionary Baines, though, challenges Tieng-Bin to view his position in the world differently by teaching him a word that does not exist in Chinese.

BAINES: In mission school, where learn me Chinese—they make—um, um—
  invent—new Chinese word, for new idea. Word is: individual.
TIENG-BIN: "Individual"?
BAINES: Meaning, each man, stand alone, choose own life. (34)[40]

In order to demonstrate the concept of the individual, Baines teaches Tieng-Bin to brag about himself, telling him that one's individuality comes through proclaiming the good and personal strengths in oneself. After praising himself for his feats, Tieng-Bin experiences the freedom and excitement that come with the recognition of one's individuality, admitting: "What a luxury. To speak the truth—in my own home, of all places" (35).

His embrace of the concept of individuality allows him to creep closer to embracing Christianity, but he also knows that if he does so, a dramatic change will occur in both his household and the domestic arrangement with his three wives, since Christianity allows him to have only one wife, which Luan also realizes. She uses this knowledge to her advantage by wearing Western clothing and being the only wife to attend the religious meetings with Baines. And yet, Tieng-Bin does not want Luan as his sole wife, favoring Eling instead. However, the closer he comes to converting to Christianity, the more Eling protests, as she views conversion to the Western faith as being a betrayal.

ELING: You want me to abandon my parents? Let their spirits wander alone
  for eternity? And if I went away with you, First Wife would lose such
  face. Is that what's best for us? To forget about others, and think only
  about ourselves?

TIENG-BIN: I thought you wanted to be modern.

ELING: I do. But does that mean I can no longer be Chinese? (45)

Eling's question identifies the issue at stake with the changes Tieng-Bin wants to institute and, in a larger sense, ties into Hwang's own question generated by the *Miss Saigon* controversy. What precisely identifies one's cultural and ethnic identity? If one becomes Christian, does that mean one is no longer Chinese? If one accepts aspects of the West, does that mean one is no longer from the East? From Eling's perspective, by embracing Christianity she rejects not only her family but also her identity as a Chinese woman. Eling's identity has been founded on these tenets all her life. As Tieng-Bin strikes down each identifying signifier with the changes he institutes, she finds that she no longer has a clear understand of self. Tieng-Bin, despite the protests he hears, decides to embrace Christianity and, with it, the worship of his wives.

With the change, though, comes devastating loss. As the baptism ceremony takes place, Siu-Yong commits suicide in her room, refusing to throw off her past and valuing it more than her husband's newfound individuality. Eling feels obligated to go through with the ceremony because of all her husband has done for her. She apologizes to her parents at their altar: "I have to do this for my Husband. He saved not only me, but all your children, from poverty and hunger" (55). However, shortly after the baptism she dies in childbirth, encouraged to accept death by the ghost of Siu-Yong, who tells her of her family's fall into slavery in the afterworld after her conversion. With the death of two of his wives, Tieng-Bin is left with Luan as his Christian wife. He sees this ignominious pairing as the final proof of his individualism, and he completely disavows his connections to the East. He reproaches his dead parents: "This is how you punish a disobedient son? Take from me the wife I love, even the wife I respect, leaving me with the one for whom I feel . . . nothing. I don't give a damn anymore about the living or the dead. Yes, by embracing the West, I have finally become . . . an individual" (59).

Hwang's intention as he wrote the play was to present a much more balanced look at religion than he had in *Family Devotions* and *Rich Relations*. The ending of the play, though, suggests that Christianity brings only destruction and suffering, in this case striking down two wives and Tieng-Bin and Eling's child, devastating a household and trampling over tradition. Hardly what one would term a fair and balanced portrayal. However, Hwang provides a coda that provides balance to the family's situation. While it is true that Tieng-Bin and his generation experience troubles throughout the conversion, the younger generation, as represented by Ahn, represents the good that can come after the turmoil and disruption. As the play switches back to the present, Andrew sees only the suffering caused by Tieng-Bin's movement to Western values. Ahn corrects him: "No. He suffer to bring family into future. Where better life, I am able to live. I first girl in family go school, choose own husband—and all the time, worship Jesus" (61).

For Ahn, the change is a positive one, leading to a far superior life than she would have had if her father had not embraced Christianity. In effect, her father's decisions allow Andrew to be in his current position in the United States, with an impending birth on the way. In order for freedom to occur, there must be suffering, and, for Ahn, the choice by her father to embrace Western ways gives her a freedom she never would have experienced otherwise. As Hwang himself explained: "The Chinese-ethnic line would be that my great-grandfather completely sold out his ethnic heritage by adopting this foreign religion. But I think there are perfectly valid reasons why Tieng-Ben does what he does, and there are both wonderful and horrible things that come out of it."[41] Ultimately, it comes down to one's interpretation of Tieng-Bin's choices and their consequences. Unlike his previous depictions of Christianity, with *Golden Child* Hwang asserts that Tieng-Bin makes the correct decisions, depicting for the first time in his work positive outcomes from the Christian faith.

CHAPTER 6

A Musical Hwang

Flower Drum Song

While Hwang is best known for his dramatic works, his childhood involvement with music provided the perfect groundwork for his involvement with musicals and operas. Hwang has admitted that, with his background, "I'm comfortable around music" and that comfort "make[s] it a kind of natural fit for me to work on productions that involve music."[1] His musical productions have been plentiful. In addition to three books for Broadway musicals, he has written numerous opera librettos, becoming the most-produced American librettist for opera.

His most consistent collaborator has been Philip Glass, with whom he has worked for more than twenty-five years. Their first collaboration, which included visuals by Jerome Sirlin, occurred in 1988 with *1000 Airplanes on the Roof,* which detailed a man's interactions with extraterrestrials. In 1992 they reteamed for *The Voyage,* which was written in honor of the five hundredth anniversary of Columbus's arrival in the Americas. In 2003 they wrote the opera version of *Sound and Beauty,* and in 2010 they created *Icarus at the Edge of Time,* which Hwang cowrote with the author Brian Greene, upon whose book the opera was based. Why has Hwang continued his partnership with Glass for so long, longer than any of his other partnerships in the theater? Hwang explained: "In my own work I'm interested in transformation and juxtaposing different worlds, periods of history, and even galaxies. Philip's work allows those transformations and juxtapositions to happen seamlessly."[2] In addition to Glass, Hwang has worked with myriad composers, including Lucia Hwong, who composed the music for a number of his early plays, including *M. Butterfly.* He wrote the libretto to Hwong's

Venus Voodoo, even playing the electric violin for its 1989 performance. He also wrote the libretto to *The Silver River* for the composer Bright Sheng; the piece premiered at the Sante Fe Chamber Music Festival in 1998. In 2003 *Ainadamar,* which featured music by Osvaldo Golijov and a libretto by Hwang, had its premiere at Tanglewood in Massachusetts. Two other librettos written in the 2000s had their premieres in Europe: Lewis Carroll's *Alice in Wonderland,* which he cowrote with the composer Unsuk Chin and which premiered in Munich in 2007, and *The Fly,* based on David Cronenberg's film, with music by Howard Shore, who also scored the movie, which had its premiere in Paris in 2008.

In terms of commercial theater, Hwang was hired to fix the book for Disney's *Aida,* which featured music and lyrics by Elton John and Tim Rice. The musical had a troubled opening in Atlanta in 1997, including a problematic book by Linda Woolverton and a malfunctioning set. Hwang reworked the musical's book for its reboot in Chicago in 1999. After this successful restart, the piece moved to Broadway in 2000 for an extended run, eventually having more than 1,800 performances. After the success of *Aida,* Disney rehired Hwang, this time to create the book for the Broadway version of *Tarzan,* which had Phil Collins, who had written the music for the movie, as its composer. It premiered in 2006, but its production was not as successful as *Aida:* its run fell short of five hundred performances. However, *Tarzan*'s shortened run on Broadway did not affect its success in Europe. As of this writing, the German production is still playing after opening in 2008.

Flower Drum Song

Despite all the operas and musical theater pieces with which he has been involved, perhaps Hwang's most significant work stemmed from his decision to revive one of Richard Rodgers and Oscar Hammerstein's less-often performed musicals, *Flower Drum Song.* Hwang was inspired to start this creative process after seeing the 1996 Broadway revival of Rodgers and Hammerstein's *The King and I.* What was so distinct about the revival and caught Hwang's interest (as well as the praise of reviewers) was the production's decision to highlight the cultural practices of Siam. Hwang thereafter asked himself what other Rodgers and Hammerstein revivals he would want to see. Immediately he thought of the oft-neglected *Flower Drum Song,* which was based on C. Y. Lee's novel of the same name. He felt that the all-Asian character musical, which ran for more than six hundred performances on Broadway in 1958, was due for a revival.

The success of *Flower Drum Song* surprised Rodgers and Hammerstein because their most recent musicals had struggled to find an audience. They had begun to surmise that they had fallen out of touch with the audience of the 1950s. The subject matter of *Flower Drum Song* also made the musical financially risky because of its exclusive focus on an Asian American community in San Francisco and its requirement of an Asian American cast. And yet, the New York audience embraced the production, making it a big enough hit that Hollywood turned it into a 1961 film.[3] The musical then mostly disappeared from American stages for two reasons: the show's requirement of Asian American performers who were triple threats—singing, dancing, and acting—made casting difficult, and the piece had become dated in its stereotypical depictions of Asian Americans as owners of laundromats, consumers of strange foods, and, in some cases, speakers of pidgin English. Instead of being performed in theatrical productions, the show's legacy became connected with the film version. Hwang wondered whether he could update the 1950s musical and help it achieve the same level of recognition as other more recognized Rodgers and Hammerstein pieces, such as *Oklahoma!, South Pacific,* and *The Sound of Music.*

The successful playwright Hwang, who was in his early forties and saw the commercial, artistic and cultural potential in a revival of *Flower Drum Song,* was at odds with his younger self, who had a much more complicated relationship with the material. When he was in his teens, he first saw the film version on television and was entranced because the film presented Asian American characters that differed from the demeaning stereotypes prevalent in movies and television programs. In the film Chinese Americans were allowed to fall in love, sing songs, tell jokes, and, perhaps more important, be full-fledged Americans. However, that early wonder and enjoyment of the piece later turned to collegiate protest. As a student at Stanford, he and a number of students took umbrage at a production of the play in San Francisco because of its stereotyped depictions of Asian Americans, especially the immigrant father and daughter. He explained: "There was great interest at that time in portraying the social ills of Chinatown, instead of doing what one Asian scholar called *State Fair* in yellow face. . . . The show was perceived as this very cheery look at what was ostensibly an Asian-American community, when that community was trying to rid itself of its false image. So it was a logical thing for us to react against it."[4] More specifically, "We thought it ignored the poverty and the tuberculosis in the Chinese-American community."[5] However, in looking back, he realized his own complicated relationship with the musical: "Along with other writers of color, we Asian-Americans sought to define our own identities, rather than permitting those images to be drawn by mainstream society, which had done such a poor job of portraying us in my youth. As part of this movement, we rather simplistically condemned virtually all portrayals of Asian-Americans created by non-Asians. So I ended up protesting *Flower Drum Song* as 'inauthentic,' though the show remained a guilty pleasure for many of us."[6] Driving his change of perspective in the late 1990s was his own two-decades-long career as a playwright and his desire to capture the Asian American and Asian immigrant experience. Perhaps the best bridge between the divergent opinions he held of the play as his younger self and as his older self was his admission that he did not "think Rodgers and Hammerstein succeeded in creating an authentic Chinese American view of life. . . . But making Asian Americans seem just as American as the characters in *Oklahoma!* is a much more innovative choice."[7]

Rewriting the musical would give Hwang the opportunity to address the issues he had criticized while in college and to incorporate his own themes, namely the assimilation of Chinese immigrants into the Asian American community and the cultural clash between East and West. In the latter case, Hwang would once again use Chinese opera, but, instead of embedding it as a theatrical device within a straight play, he would now incorporate the form into an American musical: "It seemed to me that the collision between the two could symbolize some of the central issues and disputes in the piece."[8] Hwang also saw an opportunity to unite a community of Asian American generations through this production, specifically the generation from the 1950s and early 1960s that looked fondly at the piece; Hwang's own generation, which protested against it; and a new generation of Asian Americans that might not even be aware of the musical. The significance of the new production and its unifying vision was not lost on the cast. Tzi Ma, who reunited with Hwang for *Flower Drum Song*, expressed the importance of the revised piece for Asian Americans: "When I was a kid in Staten Island—my dad owned a restaurant—I grew up on Charlie Chan and Fu Manchu and dragon ladies and Chinese people speaking funny in movies, and it was horrifying. The stereotypes were everywhere. So we don't look at *Flower Drum* as just another show. It's beyond that. It's about Asian Americans by an Asian American. The cast is Asian American. It's a monumental experience for all of us."[9]

Before he could rewrite the musical, though, he had to approach the Rodgers and Hammerstein estate for permission. Because of Hwang's strength as a Tony Award–winning playwright and because *Flower Drum Song* had become a neglected part of the Rodgers and Hammerstein canon, the estate gave Hwang carte blanche to rework the piece for a contemporary audience. Excited by their approval, Hwang "tried to write the book that Oscar Hammerstein would have written had he been Asian-American."[10] However, when Hwang turned in his first draft, it was, according to Ted Chapin, who ran the estate, "totally unproduceable."[11] His draft revolved around a number of San Francisco's ethnic neighborhoods, including a major plot point involving Italians. Even more problematic was what Hwang had done with the songs, breaking them up and sprinkling them throughout the text. Later, Hwang admitted to the problems he created with this first attempt at the new book, explaining that "I had gone into this project with some arrogance, not having bothered to school myself in the very specific craft of musical book writing."[12] To aid Hwang, the estate brought in director Robert Longbottom and musical director David Chase. For the next two years the three worked together, shaping the piece into its final musical theatrical form. Hwang revealed that not a single line of the original libretto, cowritten by Hammerstein and Joseph Fields, existed in the new version. Because of the songs, they decided to maintain the setting as the late 1950s; this time overlapped advantageously with the heyday of the Chop Suey Circuit for Asian performers, which became the focus for the new story line. In addition, maintaining the original time period assisted with some of the more problematic songs, which were dated and considered by some to be offensive. To solve the problem, songs like "Chop Suey" were turned into performative pieces set on the stage of the theater, allowing them to blend into the story more smoothly and believably for contemporary audiences. They also reworked the meaning of some songs by changing their context and, in turn, the character's motivation for singing the song. Finally, they restored "My Best Love," which had been cut from the original Broadway show, and moved "The Next Time It Happens" from Rodgers and Hammerstein's *Pipe Dream* into the production.

Before opening on Broadway, the musical premiered in Los Angeles at the Mark Taper Forum. Because an investor failed to make a deadline, however, the producers had to scale back the production, moving it from its intended 2,000-seat auditorium into a more intimate 750-seat theater and reducing the musical accompaniment to six musicians. Surprisingly, the originally unplanned intimacy helped reinforce the theatrical component of the revived production. *Flower Drum Song* transferred to Broadway, where it opened at the Virginia Theatre on October 17, 2002. After a run of only 169 performances, it closed early. It later received three Tony nominations, including one for Hwang for best book but failed to win.

C. Y. Lee, the author of the novel, was asked why he thought *Flower Drum Song* did so poorly in New York in comparison to its successful run in Los Angeles. He pinpointed the reason for the failure as the *New York Times*, repeating a criticism stated by many others about the newspaper's power over the lifespan of theatrical productions. When Hwang began his career,

Frank Rich of the *New York Times* was complimentary and supportive of the majority of his plays (*Rich Relations* being the exception). However, Rich became a columnist, and his replacement, Ben Brantley, was not as kind to Hwang's plays. In his review Brantley admitted that there were "honorable intentions behind the creative team's effort to resuscitate a work regarded as terminally out of date" and noted that Hwang's affection for the musical was apparent. And yet, one of Brantley's main criticisms of the play concerned Hwang's characterizations of his Asian American characters. Brantley felt that they flopped because the play "strain[s] in transforming cute and cozy ethnic types from the Broadway production of 1958 into a set of positive Asian role models that might be introduced into a public school presentation in 2002." The characters were far too one-dimensional and spoke as if they were in a sitcom (Brantley compared Hwang's dialogue to the dialogue in the TV shows *Three's Company* and *Will and Grace*). Charles Isherwood of *Variety* was equally dubious about the revival, calling it a "painstaking reinvention." While Isherwood believed that "Hwang has done a fine job of creating a more clarified storyline, and they've smoothly integrated all but one of the original songs into a plot that now only tangentially resembles the original," it still did not fix the problems with the book, which was "a compendium of cardboard characters and corny jokes." Michael Feingold of the *Village Voice* was equally unimpressed, calling the musical "historically iffy and dramatically tenuous" and terming the entire project a "Hwangian farrago."[13]

Other reviewers though liked the musical, including John Lahr of *The New Yorker,* who wrote that Hwang "puts a new chassis on an old engine. He eliminates stereotype, updates the evergreen American-immigrant dilemma over traditional and contemporary values, and repositions some of the songs as segues to more sophisticated, multicultural themes. The result is a vehicle that runs far better than its prototype." He cited Hwang as besting the musical duo of Rodgers and Hammerstein because the strength of his story and Mei-li's characterization meant that "one is more aware of the weakness of the music." Perhaps the most enthusiastic reception for the play came from Richard Zoglin, *Time*'s reviewer, who listed the production as one of the ten best of the year and enthusiastically raved: "*Flower Drum Song* has been rescued from the dustbin of theater history and made relevant again without getting weighed down by political correctness. This new Broadway revival is a work of bravery and intelligence and real faith in the possibilities of musical theater." In addition, the play is "a richer, more nuanced exploration of the immigrant experience."[14] While C. Y. Lee saw the review from the *New York Times* as the death of the show, another factor contributing to its early close was that it opened only a year after the terrorist attacks of September 11, 2001; audiences and tourists had still not yet returned to New York in their pre-September 11 numbers. While there was discussion of a travelling production of the show, it never materialized.

Rodgers and Hammerstein's *Flower Drum Song* follows the travails of Mei-li, a Chinese immigrant, who has come to San Francisco as an arranged bride for Sammy Fong, who has eyes only for Linda Low, one of the performers in his nightclub. Fong hoists Mei-li on another Chinese family that is seeking a spouse for a son, Wang Ta, who also happens to be in love with Linda Low. Throughout the course of the musical Wang Ta grows to have feelings for Mei-li, and by the end of the piece a double wedding occurs for Mei-li and Wang and Sammy and Linda. In the larger narrative sense, Hwang's play is similar. While he drops the character of Sammy, he maintains the love triangle among Mei-li, Ta, and Linda Low. In addition, he creates a subplot surrounding the successful reincarnation of the theater owned by Wang, Ta's father, who relishes the opportunity to perform before adoring crowds. After Mei-li and Ta have a falling out, Mei-li threatens to return to China with Chao, another immigrant, but Ta convinces her to stay in San Francisco, and the musical ends with their marriage.

The musical's opening establishes that the immigrant experience of Mei-li is more harrowing than that of her 1950s predecessor. Using "One Hundred Million Miracles," perhaps the best-known song from the production, in the prologue, Hwang counters the optimistic lyrics with a depiction of the turbulent conditions in China as Mei-li watches her father get arrested for his angry protest against Mao Zedong and the Communists. She then, at her father's urging, leaves China and travels in miserable conditions as she and other immigrants make their way across the Pacific in the hull of a ship. Hwang used a similar image in Ma's opera sequence in *The Dance and the Railroad,* suggesting that not much has changed from the mid-nineteenth century to the mid-twentieth century for Chinese immigrants seeking a new start in the United States. While the song extols the wonders of miracles happening every day, the ironic reality of Mei-li and the other Chinese immigrants' experience suggests the absence of miracles in China or on their cramped journey to a possible release from their troubled homeland. Their only hope of a miracle resides in their destination: America. Interspersed with the lyrics of the song are the wishes of the immigrants in the hull of the boat for a better future in America.

REFUGEE #1 (Chao): Though my body crosses the ocean in this cramped tomb, I keep my mind fixed on my new life to come.

REFUGEE #2: My child will be born in America, and will grow up without fear, for she will know neither famine nor war.[15]

The immigrants' expectations of America are far more tempered than Ma's grandiose expectation of the Gold Mountain. Some of the immigrants in *Flower Drum Song* will find happiness in their new country, and some, like Chao above, will leave, not having found the success they had imagined.

As mentioned earlier, Hwang set the musical within the theater, allowing him to highlight again the cultural differences between East and West, this time in terms of Chinese and Western theater. Mei-li comes across the club where Ta and his father, Wang, perform Chinese opera for a few scattered ticketholders. In order to make ends meet, Wang allows Ta to use the theater as a nightclub a few nights a week, and the club is highly successful. The Westernized, assimilated Ta, who was born in China but came to America when he was two, wants to embrace fully the capitalistic opportunities available through the success of his nightclub by opening up on more evenings, but his father keeps him chained to Chinese tradition through their poorly attended performances of stories from the Old Country. Mei-li immediately notices the nature of Ta's struggle between what his father wants for him and his own desires, telling him:

MEI-LI: Ta, sometimes you seem a hundred percent Chinese. Then a moment later, you become a hundred percent American.
TA: So what does that make me? A hundred percent nothing?
MEI-LI: No. I think you are . . . a hundred percent both. (20)

Even though Mei-li sees and understands, like many of Hwang's characters before her, the necessity of being able to blend the old with the new, the East with the West, tradition with change, Ta, like Dale in *FOB,* openly disdains Chinese culture, which becomes apparent when Mei-li, who is also trained in Chinese opera, auditions for him. He tells her: "First you do the mincing walk, then the stupid pose, then the nauseating giggle. Got it?" (19). His lack of respect for his culture and his father's cultural ties to China is embedded not just in his insulting descriptions of the dance moves but also in his disdain for the myths the operas enact.

TA: The love of a beautiful maiden turns a humble scholar into a god. Sounds credible to me.
MEI-LI: Ta, the Flower Boat Maiden does not turn the scholar into a god. He has always been a god. Only he has forgotten that he came originally from heaven. (32)

This contrast is one of the causes of their romantic struggles. Both characters want to succeed in America, but their concepts of success differ. Mei-li just wants to escape the hardships suffered in China, finding companionship and community in her new country while maintaining her ties to Chinese tradition. Ta, though, wants all the trappings of success, mostly monetary, promised by the American dream

Mei-li's earnest and passionate defense of their Chinese culture and their connection to their birthplace finally begins to have an effect on Ta, and, despite Ta's attempts to distance himself from his Chinese heritage through insults and disdainful comments, he does finally admit that part of his identity is tied to the East. This aspect of his identity becomes apparent when both share stories about the loss of a parent.

MEI-LI: My father was arrested by the Communists—and died in prison. Before he went away, he whispered to me, "Take this drum, Daughter— and never stop dreaming. For the more you dream, the more miracles you will see."
TA: My mother died on the boat, coming to America. I was only two. (32)

Both associate their freedom and the opportunities they enjoy in their new country with the death of a parent, who committed the greatest sacrifice possible to help a child. Eventually, Mei-li's ability to bridge the two cultures helps Ta appreciate the importance of these Chinese stories and histories in terms of what they mean to his identity as well as his cultural connection with others in Chinatown. Just as Grace instructed Steve in *FOB*, to be successful in the great melting pot one must be able to coexist in both worlds and appreciate what both cultures have to offer, finding a comfortable space within old and new, tradition and experiment, community and individuality.

Paralleling *FOB*, Hwang frames the relationship between Ta and Mei-li through a love triangle, but in this case he uses two love triangles. The first one involves Ta, Mei-li, and Linda Low, who is another significant force behind Ta's desire to reject his Chinese heritage and become fully Americanized because she dates only white men. He wants Linda to break her rule, to be attracted to him as much she is to the Caucasian men she dates. However, as Ta's father says, it is impossible for Ta to be seen in such a way by Linda. How can she see him as attractive, since even "the Americans will never accept him in their country" (23)? He will always be seen as an outsider. Ta presses Linda on why she instituted such a rule on her love life. She explains: "For the same reason you always hated doing Chinese opera. We all wanna be Americans—like everyone else. (*Pause.*) When I'm out with my boyfriends,

no one ever says to me, 'Go back to where you came from.' Is that so terrible? To feel now and then like I actually belong here?" (86).

Linda's comment recalls a subject that Hwang explored in *Bondage* with
Mark and the prejudices he faced from non-Asians. To combat such prejudicial remarks Linda has taken the opportunity to craft an entire new persona.
She confesses to Ta that she was not born Linda Low. She actually changed
her name, which used to be Low Lee-Fung, to make it more American. Linda's rejection of her Chinese name and thus her identity allowed her to refuse
to accept her place as a traditional Chinese woman. By becoming Linda Low,
she can still make a living in Chinatown performing, but privately she can
become like any other non-Asian woman in America. To help enhance her
passing, she wears only Western clothes, whereas Mei-li wear only Chinese
outfits, which Linda cattily dismisses: "I guess this is sorta sexy—if you have
a thing for Chinese grandmothers" (24). Mei-li sees how Linda's bearing and
assimilation to the West attract the eye of Ta, and she later accepts Linda's
offer to dress her in Western clothes so that she too can attract his attention.
However, Ta rejects Mei-li's causing a rift in their friendship.

TA: You look beautiful. It's not the dress.
MEI-LI: Then it's me you don't want, isn't it? Someone fresh off the boat,
   who doesn't know how to dress, or wear her hair—
TA: I—
MEI-LI: You're right, Ta, I don't fit in here. I'm just some foolish refugee—
   who thought you kissed me . . . because you loved me. (60)

The failure of the dress to catch his attention provokes the two to separate
and shatters Mei-li's first love affair.

After running away from the theater, Mei-li reconnects with Chao, who
crossed over with her on the boat. He helps her find work in a factory, far
from the glamorous work of the theater. Chao plans to save his earnings to
return to China, dismissing the drawing power of America and repelled by
the actions of his fellow Chinese making their way in the United States. He
tells Mei-Li, after she tries to defend their fellow countrymen: "They live a
little better than we do. And try so hard to fit in, they don't even know who
they are no more. I'm a practical man. And it's never gonna happen for me
over here" (76). Chao's presence in the play and his interchange with Mei-li,
according to Dan Bacalzo, demonstrates Hwang's success at "capturing the
conflicted feelings of new Asian immigrants as they try to find their place
in the U.S.A."[16] As in *FOB*, Hwang creates a romantic triangle between a
woman and two disparate men representing different views of America and

of their Chinese identity. As Grace faced a choice between Steve and Dale, Hwang now has Mei-li facing the two differing philosophies of Chao and Ta. Chao represents the siren's call of China, hard work and a government that killed her father. In addition, Chao shows a lack of respect for her by forcing her to pawn her flower drum, given to her by her father, in order to speed up their savings so that they can return to China. Ta represents the call of San Francisco and America, which is unpredictable, filled with unfamiliar values and culture, and the land of opportunity and freedom. In addition, Ta has come to respect Mei-li and understand her values; he buys the flower drum from the pawn shop where Chao hawked it and returns it to her, proving his love for her. Just as in *FOB*, Mei-li's choice is not surprising, as she chooses Ta, and the musical ends with them happily performing Chinese opera to a small group of audience members.

While members of the younger generation struggle with their romantic relationships infused with questions of what it means to be American, those of the older generation, represented by Wang, Ta's father, and Liang, a talent agent, turn Wang's anemic theater into a successful member of the profitable Chop Suey Circuit. Liang changes the name of Wang's struggling theater from the Golden Pearl to Club Chop Suey. Her intention is to raise the status of the Chinese in America. In essence, what Linda Low accomplished on an individual level, converting herself into an American and moving away from her Chinese roots, Laing wants to do for the entire Chinese American community. She sees Chinatown as being part of the problem: "Master Wang, when the average American thinks of Chinatown, do you know what they imagine? Opium dens, Tong wars, female slavery and questionable cuts of meat" (35). Just as Linda says she wants to be an American, Liang believes the Chinese have to embrace the same ideal. They have to transform their Asian identity and reject the stereotypes and expectations prevalent among the non-Asian American populace. She exhorts: "We've got to show the Americans who we really are. No more inscrutable Orientals, but smiling, all American faces. Polite men, beautiful women, the finest cuisine in the world" (36). Chinese people should no longer be seen as outsiders. They need to be viewed as insiders, just like everyone else. Wang's theater offers the opportunity to promote this change. At first Wang, citing tradition and the importance of their heritage, is none too pleased with Liang's changes to his theater and with the primarily Caucasian audience whooping it up and enjoying themselves in his previously staid and serious space. He rails at her: "This mob has come only to have a good time. In China, none of my audiences ever expected to have a good time! I have half a mind to toss them all out of here. This is no longer my theatre" (51). However, Wang, despite his outward distress, is a performer at heart, and when he performs in front of the raucous crowd and receives applause and accolades for his performance, which he did not receive for his Chinese opera performances, he, like Linda before him, suddenly sees a great performance opportunity before him. He transforms himself from an artist from the old country, set in his ways of proper Eastern performance, to a major ham, seeking the limelight and applause and performing in comical musical pieces like "Chop Suey," with dancers in Chinese To Go boxes, and creating a comical Confucius-like character.

WANG: I come out as: Master Confucius, Ancient Oriental Wiseguy.
TA: You guys ever think we might be going just a bit too far?
WANG (*As Confucius*): Confucius say, "Two whites don't make a Wong."
    (*As himself*) What do you mean, "too far"?
TA: What happened to the "New Chinatown"?
LIANG: Sure, we'll give the tourists what they want, but we'll have the last laugh. (68)

Wang disavows his obligations to his Chinese past to worship instead at the altar of applause from the audience. He proceeds to hijack the show, placing himself as the main performer. With this fulfilling of Western stereotypes of the East, he drops the subtle art of movement and storytelling of the East and instead accepts the crass, one-dimensional nature of what passes for Western entertainment. While the stories he performed from the Chinese opera represented millennia of Chinese history, the pieces he performs on the circuit completely undercut and dismantle the importance and significance of his culture. He used to tell stories about gods but now enacts stereotypes replete with pidgin English and allusions to bad Chinese food. However, Wang does explain his rationale for the dramatic change in temperament when he speaks to his dead wife, telling her: "You know how hard I tried. But I couldn't get them to love our opera here—I couldn't even convince our own son. And you know how much I love the sound of an audience. So can you please forgive me, that I have finally begun to find happiness?" (71). While it is an honest moment from Wang, it also reveals his shallowness and makes clear that his desires are more important than tradition. And yet, through his success, he has fulfilled Liang's goal of helping Chinese Americans become true Americans. Wang, after all, instills in himself the American principle of the self before everything else, especially when it comes to his own happiness. Applause, ego, and money help him achieve the American dream. While Wang has found his own reward in embracing these elements, Ta, who at first worshipped these very same elements, now has, through Mei-li's assistance, found happiness in what Wang abandoned, the stories from his country's past. As in *The Dance and the Railroad,* the two men switch places and, in doing so, find contentment in Chinatown and America. No matter where and how the characters have achieved their dreams, they have found their place in the United States.

And yet, it is worth returning to the ways Wang achieves his happiness. He does so through the reification of Asian stereotypes, especially in regard to the joke-telling Confucius role he creates. In a sense, Wang appears to be selling out his heritage and community by promulgating such stereotypes. Such behavior clearly undermines the role of Asian Americans in the play, and, as noted in the reviews of the play, some critics took Hwang to task for the musical's exaggerated stereotypes. However, Hwang's position about his deliberate use of stereotypes is much more nuanced and embedded in the history of Chinese Americans in the 1950s, which is when the play is set. Addressing the issue of stereotypes, Hwang told the story of two members of the original Chop Suey Circuit, who performed on *The Ed Sullivan Show.* When the husband-and-wife team stepped before the cameras, they wore traditional Chinese clothing and spoke in halting English, but then all of a sudden the couple surprised the audience by taking off their clothes revealing a tuxedoed man and a woman wearing a ball dress, who proceeded to dance in a Western style. Hwang asked, How do we respond to such a presentation? He revealed that the performers believed "they were subverting the societal stereotypes of their day. I have come to embrace that explanation; you cannot necessarily judge attitudes of earlier eras by today's standards. Moreover, I began to realize that one generation's breakthroughs often become the next generation's stereotypes."[17] The two performers on *The Ed Sullivan Show* fooled their American audience by first embodying the stereotypical signifiers of Chinese immigrants in order to disrupt that expectation through the flawless performance of an American dance routine, reminiscent of Fred Astaire and Ginger Rogers; thus, in the space of a few minutes they challenged an Asian stereotype by transforming it into an iconic American image, confronting their audience's prejudices and preconceptions about Asians in American. Wang's performance works similarly. As Liang says to Ta's question about his father's Confucius skit, "we will have the last laugh." Previously, their neighborhood had been viewed with disdain and disrespect. The performances of the Chop Suey Circuit allow the interaction of non-Asians and Asians to occur in an environment controlled by the Asians, rather than by the societal prejudices created by non-Asians. In turn, the members of the Chop Suey Circuit empower themselves by laughing at themselves and allow others to laugh with them. The previous stereotypes of Asians are then demolished by the professional theatrical productions and their ability to entertain.

Hwang uses a similar device on his twenty-first-century audience at the play's end. After they are married, Mei-li and Ta give thanks:

MEI-LI: As I begin my new life, I give thanks to all those who came before me. My father . . .

TA: . . . my mother, and their ancestors before them . . .

MEI-LI: . . . whose legacy was passed down to me the day I was born (*Turns to face the audience*) in Soochow, China.

TA: (*Turns to face the audience*) The day I was born—in Shanghai.

(*As each of the following speak, they step forward to address the audience:*)

LINDA: The day I was born—in Seattle.

WANG: In Hunan, China.

HARVARD: In Stockton, California.

LIANG: In New York City.

(*Each member of the ensemble now states the actual place of his or her birth.*) (96–97)

While the actors playing the main figures remain in character as they reveal their birthplaces, in a bit of theatrical ingenuity the ensemble suddenly transforms from their Hwang-created selves into their real selves. The characters they have played, the stereotypes they have embraced as characters, the jokes they have told, the crowd-pleasing songs they have sung are now in a Brechtian moment dismissed as the characters become real-life performers who announce to the audience where they were born. In setting up this change, Hwang shows the complexity of identity and nationality when it comes to Asian faces. One cannot surmise a person's history and sense of self from just a glance at a face. The actors have taken different journeys to reach this point on this Broadway stage in front of this audience on this night, and their experiences link all of them. In this moment the musical is no longer simply a revision of the Rodgers and Hammerstein musical. Instead, it is a larger comment about the Asian and Asian American journey traveled by the *Flower Drum Song* story itself from its first incarnation as a novel by C. Y. Lee to the Broadway musical to the Hollywood film to Hwang's rewritten version. The announcement of their birthplaces, which ranges from Hong Kong and Japan to Canada and the United States, also provides a connection to the actors who came before and performed *Flower Drum Song*, highlighting America's reliance on new immigrants as well as on those who have taken root in the country to tell its stories and celebrate its history.

CHAPTER 7

Wrapping Up, Beginning Anew
Yellow Face and *Chinglish*

For the 1996 Humana Festival in Louisville, Kentucky, Hwang wrote *Trying to Find Chinatown,* a short play that explores the complexity of defining authentic ethnic identity, especially when that identity is determined by one's appearance. The play would be one of a number of pieces that would be a precursor to *Yellow Face.* In *Trying to Find Chinatown* Ronnie, an Asian American male busker, plays his violin on the streets of New York. Benjamin, a Caucasian man, asks for directions to a Chinatown residence, which angers Ronnie, who accuses Benjamin of being racist because he asked an Asian man where Chinatown was, assuming that an Asian would automatically know. Benjamin, though, surprises Ronnie with his response: "Brother, I can absolutely relate to your anger. Righteous rage, I suppose, would be a more appropriate term. To be marginalized, as we are, by a white racist patriarchy, to the point where the accomplishments of our people are obliterated from the history books, this is cultural genocide of the first order, leading to the fact that you must do battle with all of Euro-America's emasculating and brutal stereotypes of Asians."[1] Benjamin reveals that he was adopted by an Asian American family and raised in a Chinese American community, which provided him with a far more authentic and profound Chinese background than Ronnie has. Benjamin identifies Ronnie as "one of those self-hating, *assimilated* Chinese-Americans, aren't you?" (291). However, at the heart of the play is a concept in which Hwang had become much more invested when it came to identity. As Benjamin tells Ronnie: "Well, you can't judge my race by my genetic heritage alone" (290). Benjamin's situation as a Caucasian adopted into an Asian household, a reversal of Caucasians adopting Asian babies, challenges the false assumptions and prejudices tied to appearance, which Hwang began to explore in *Bondage*. After all, how much does one's skin color really reveal about a person? Hwang answered: "We have these mythologies that skin color should mean certain things, that we can gain information about the essence of a person by observing certain things in their exterior. I don't know that that's necessarily true, because a lot of times what would be information that you infer from looking at someone's outward features may be completely at odds with what their interior actually holds."[2]

Hwang explored the same idea again in 2001 in another short play, *Jade Flowerpots and Bound Feet,* written for *The Square,* a project commissioned by the Mark Taper Forum and compiled by Lisa Peterson and Chay Yew that explored the Asian American experience from the Civil War to the present. Once again in this play Hwang examines the authenticity of true cultural identity contrasted with appearance. In the ten-minute play a woman, Kwok Mei-Li, has written a memoir about her Asian American upbringing. When she comes to visit her African American editor, she is told that the company will not publish her story because of her Caucasian appearance. The author is then forced by her editor to reveal that Kwok Mei-Li is actually her writing name and that she was born Ashley Winterstone. Mei-Li makes a compelling argument against simple ethnic signifiers: "You know . . . has it ever occurred to you—that even a work written by someone who's 100 percent non-Asian might be authentic? Or, that one written by a full-blooded Asian might not be? What if the book by the non-Asian was better?"[3] The play ends with the editor calling for Mei-Li to submit to a blood test to ensure that she is truly Asian (she claims to be a quarter Asian). These two short plays allowed Hwang to experiment with the intricate question of authentic ethnicity in smaller venues with lowered audience expectations (just as he did with *Bondage*) in order to hone his message and dramatic exploration before once again taking on the topic in the full-length play *Yellow Face.*

Yellow Face

The failure of *Face Value* stayed with Hwang throughout the 1990s and into the 2000s. *Yellow Face* came into being because "I'd been wanting to fix my play *Face Value* for the past 17 years, but I couldn't figure out how to do it. Then I started thinking about the stage documentary form—making it a mock stage documentary that would poke fun at some of the absurdities of the multicultural movement."[4] The stage documentary form had been used quite successfully for American plays such as Moisés Kaufman's *The Laramie Project,* which looked at the murder of Matthew Shepard, and for British plays, including David Hare's *The Permanent Way,* about the dismal condition of the national railway, which had resulted in fatal train crashes. Hwang saw the potential in the form, which uses public documents, interviews, and media statements as a means to dramatize a story. With *Yellow Face*, Hwang played with the form, blending real people and institutions with fictional characters and situations, thus intentionally placing the audience in a state of uncertainty about which items are authentic and which are not, an effect he had achieved through the use of masks in *Bondage*. Leigh Silverman, the director of *Yellow Face*, commented on this aspect of the play, noting that what "we ask people to believe in in the play is that everything that you're seeing is true, and everything that you're seeing is theater. And it—that it really leaves it up to the audience to decide. And I think that is part of the conception of the play, with many actors playing many different roles of different races and different genders. I think it's part of the idea of anyone can do anything, everyone can do anything."[5]

Hwang decided to make himself the main character, called DHH, but he realized that autobiographical plays, like Eugene O'Neill's *Long Day's Journey into Night* and Tennessee Williams's *The Glass Menagerie*, where the author is a character in the work, are problematic because the author's doppelganger is not as developed as the other characters. Hwang found that issue to be moot as he wrote, remarking "I found that by creating a character that I actually gave my name to, in a strange way it liberated me to make him a character. . . . It's kind of counterintuitive, but by naming him after myself he became more of a character."[6] Perhaps Hwang did not experience this difficulty because he had no ego attached to the depiction of the main character. He described DHH as "the one who makes the biggest mistakes and in some sense is the most foolish person in the play."[7] Part of the inspiration to make himself the main character as well as a comical figure stemmed from an experience he had with the film director Greg Pak, who made a short film called *Asian Pride Porn*, which features Hwang playing himself "hawking politically correct Asian porn."[8] Hwang's father, Henry, after a twenty-year absence from his son's plays, also made a return in *Yellow Face*, inspiring the character HYH. Unfortunately, his father died of cancer before the play premiered, but he did read an early version of the draft and enjoyed his son's depiction of him. Hwang reflected on his father's connection to the play before *Yellow Face*'s New York opening: "I've become more and more aware of the degree to which this is really a play that, in many ways, I'm writing kind of a tribute to my father."[9]

Once again, Hwang's latest play had its premiere outside New York, this time playing in Los Angeles at the Mark Taper Forum in May 2007 before opening off-Broadway at the Public Theater in New York on December

10, 2007. The New York theater critics were of differing opinions. Jeremy
McCarter of *New York* admitted that even though Hwang was not groundbreaking in his commentary about race or his use of metatheater, "you have
to admire Hwang's ability to keep his sense of humor while doing a difficult
thing: Motivated by an angry but heartfelt patriotism, he is challenging a
country he plainly loves." He also pointed out that the play's structure was
at times confusing and contradictory but admitted that this comment was
not necessarily a criticism, asking, "what do you expect of a serious play
about race in America?" Marilyn Stasio, writing for *Variety*, was surprised
by how much she laughed, asking in her review "since when did he turn
into such a funny guy?" and noting that the play contained "much wry,
even self-effacing humor." She found Hwang's father's alter ego, HYH, "ir-
resistible." Michael Feingold of the *Village Voice* was honestly not looking
forward to viewing the new Hwang play. As Feingold explained, it had been
ten years since *Golden Child*, and Hwang had helped fill the decade by writing the books for three musicals. Feingold felt "active dread" walking into
the theater because, in his mind, Hwang had "become American playwriting's symbol of socially approved preachiness." (Feingold especially took
great umbrage at Hwang's book for *Tarzan*.) However, Feingold's dread was
quickly replaced with glee. He found the play to be "charming, touching,
and cunningly organized as well as funny." He considered *Yellow Face* to be
"Hwang's comic atonement for his years as a political corrector." The play
served as "a mordant, reflective comedy that works not only as a personal
summation but as a pattern for us all as we pick our cautious way through
the thicket of claims and counterclaims that marks America's transactions
with its minorities."[10]

The *New York Times*, however, was not so effusive in its praise. Ben
Brantley called the piece "messy" and pointed out that it "suffers from its
own artistic identity crisis": the play, he said, covered a range of emotional
outlets from humor to anger, creating "such a radical twist in tone that it
leaves you with whiplash. It's like a late-night phone call from a friend in
crisis who begins by cracking wise and ends by sobbing convulsively." Like
Feingold, Brantley too brought up *Tarzan*, suggesting that the play suffered
from the same type of glib one-liners that dotted his script for Disney. Ultimately, the play felt like "a collage assembled in haste." Brantley noted that
it "feels less like a fully developed work than a scattershot, personal venting
of painful emotions, still waiting to assume a polished form." Frank Scheck
of the *New York Post* found the play confusing as "the playwright's incisive
points become lost in a morass of real and invented plot elements that never
quite jibe."[11] Despite the mixed reviews, *Yellow Face* was nominated for a

Pulitzer Prize, losing to Tracy Letts's *August: Osage County.* However, it won Hwang his third Obie for best play.

As the play opens, DHH involves himself with the protest over the casting of *Miss Saigon,* but when it becomes too controversial, he pulls himself out of the limelight and reneges on his fellow protesters. His focus then turns to casting an Asian actor for the lead in his new play, *Face Value,* which is based on the controversy. Late in the casting process, the producers bring in an actor from a play set during World War II about a conflicted Japanese American soldier. However, they mistakenly bring in the Caucasian co-star, Marcus G. Dahlman, rather than the actor who actually played the Asian American soldier. Even though Marcus does not have Asian features, they cast him as the lead, prompted by DHH's umbrage at the producer's concern over Marcus's non-Asian appearance. Later DHH learns that they brought in the wrong actor for the audition and that Marcus is actually Caucasian. Unable to fire Marcus because it would be against the law, DHH creates a faux Asian identity for him, claiming his Siberian roots as the basis for his Asian identity. Marcus's career as an Asian American actor blossoms as he eventually lands the lead role in *The King and I,* while DHH angrily obsesses over Marcus's success. In addition to Marcus, DHH deals with his father, HYH, who sees all bad news as good publicity, espouses his love of America, thinks *Miss Saigon* is a wonderful musical, and wants his son to get him tickets. In the second half of the play HYH comes under investigation for his bank's role in soliciting Chinese contributions in support of President Clinton's bid for re-election, and Marcus, under pressure from the government for his own contributions, admits he is not Asian. DHH notices a pattern of racial attacks against Chinese Americans and confronts a *New York Times* reporter who is investigating HYH. During the course of the interview, DHH elicits a racist comment from the reporter, which squelches the investigation into his father. The play ends with Marcus in China communing with his newly adopted country and being accepted by the residents of a Chinese village, while DHH sits alone on the stage, still seeking his own place.

For a playwright who has throughout his career been fascinated with the subject of identity in its many facets (Asian, Chinese, American, Asian American, Chinese American, male, female, religious, and familial), in *Yellow Face* Hwang explores for the first time the concept of identity as it relates to what he knows best—himself. While he has on occasion used himself as inspiration for a character, such as Chester in *Family Devotions,* this is the first time he has placed himself directly within the play as its main character, and in doing so he does not give DHH any preferential treatment. DHH is shallow, self-serving, narcissistic, porn obsessed, and an online troller for sexual hook-ups. For much of the play DHH does not stand up for himself but instead opts for the easiest way out of the dilemmas he faces. Once the media firestorm grows over the *Miss Saigon* protest, DHH immediately backs out of his anti-yellowface position. Carla Chang, an activist, argues that he should stay involved in the protest, but for Hwang, his successful playwriting face, the public persona he presents, is more important than causing a stir. For this reason he does not want to be the face of the movement. After all, he has his writing career to worry about.

CARLA CHANG: This is our Rosa Parks moment! Now, tomorrow, we
    need you to—
DHH: Why? Why do you need me?
CARLA CHANG: Because—you're a name the papers know and—
DHH: That's right, it's *my* name out there. *My* face in the papers—the
    poster child for political correctness.[12]

While DHH is invested in merely protecting himself and his continued success without causing ripples, his father, HYH, effuses about America. Even though he came to the United States as an immigrant decades ago, he still marvels at the numerous opportunities that abound. Where DHH sees only negative publicity with the *Miss Saigon* protest and, then later, the failure of *Face Value,* HYH sees only the positive side of his son's name becoming a battering ram for the right. HYH exclaims: "When I was working in a laundry, could I ever have dreamed? That one day Charlton Heston would write—about *my* son? I'm telling you, this is the land of opportunity" (14). The two then become involved in a spirited conversation about *Miss Saigon* with each Hwang espousing a different perspective. Whereas DHH sees only yellowface, HYH appreciates the larger context behind the story and its meaning to people like him. He explains to his son why the play is such a big hit.

HYH: Because it's real.
DHH: A Vietnamese prostitute falls in love with some white soldier and kills
    herself so her baby can come to America?
HYH: Things like that happen all the time.
DHH: How can you say—?
HYH: You don't know how much people want to come to America. I see
    that girl, and I think—she's like me. (16)

As an immigrant, HYH knows what life was like in China and what his life is like now in the United States. HYH can see the same passion and need for escape in the *Miss Saigon* heroine as he does in his own American immigrant experience. DHH, though, is an American-Born Chinese, born to successful

parents and raised in an affluent home. He has not known struggle and sacrifice. All he has had to worry about is himself and his reputation; he has
relied on others to look out for him, as his father does when *Face Value* flops
and his father puts him on the board of the bank to help him out financially.
Unlike his father, who came to America on his own with little to his name,
DHH has a net to protect him. HYH's identity, then, is defined through the
lens of his embracing America as his home, whereas DHH's identity is defined merely through his own selfishness.

In addition to making fun of himself, Hwang skewers Asian stereotypes,
playing up the feminine characteristics attributed to Asian males, a subject he
also tackled in *M. Butterfly*. As they struggle to cast the lead actor for *Face
Value*, DHH complains about the difficulty in finding an Asian male who
embodies the needed elements for his character.

DHH: This is our chance. To make some fresh Asian face into a Broadway
    star. For *M. Butterfly* we were looking for a Chinese transvestite who
    could sing and dance! And we found lots of them!
STUART: Yes we did.
DHH: So why is this so much harder? All we're looking for is a straight,
    masculine, Asian leading man. (18)

Of course, the irony of DHH's statement is that that when they do find
their "straight, masculine, Asian leading man," he turns out to be a straight,
masculine Caucasian man named Marcus G. Dahlman, who was in play
about a Japanese American fighting against the Japanese during World War
II. Believing he had played the Japanese American role, the casting director
has Marcus audition. Uncertain of his ethnicity because of his Caucasian appearance, the casting crew tries to divine from strategically leading questions,
since they cannot ask him directly his about ethnicity, whether or not he is
Asian. However, Marcus's enigmatic answers do not provide a firm confirmation of his ethnic identity. After he leaves the audition, the production team
debates the merits of hiring him, since Marcus lacks the usual telling Asian
facial features.

STUART: But guys, does he—? Does he look Asian to you?
DHH: What do you mean, "look Asian"?
STUART: Well, he doesn't seem to possess—any Asian features . . . at all.
DHH: And what exactly are "Asian features"?
STUART: He's got dark hair, but—
DHH: Short, high cheekbones, slanty eyes?
STUART: David—

DHH: I gotta say, I find your questions sort of offensive. Asian faces come in a variety of shapes and sizes—just like any other human beings. Which we are, you know. (21)

Keeping in character, DHH uses the claim of racism when it is convenient for his own benefit (desperately needing an actor because rehearsals begin in a few days) and not to further a larger societal goal (ending yellowface on Broadway).

Later, DHH's self-preservation mode kicks in when he learns that Marcus is actually white, which he discovers after talking to the actor who played the Japanese American soldier in the World War II play. The actor berates DHH: "Anyone else would have their balls handed back to them on a plate by our community. But fucking David Henry Hwang—*he* can cast a white guy as an Asian and no one gives a goddamn!" (26). In order to save face, rather than admit his mistake and face certain media crucifixion, DHH creates a fictional Asian identity for Marcus G. Dahlman by dropping his last name and turning his middle initial into his new surname. Farewell, Marcus G. Dahlman; hello, Marcus Gee. DHH latches on to Marcus's partial Siberian lineage to argue for his Asian ethnicity, artfully creating an ethnic identity from nothing and transforming a Caucasian into an Asian. Theatrically, it is an extremely funny moment of backpedaling and straining by DHH to save face after he has done exactly what he had criticized Cameron Mackintosh for doing. In contrast to the humor of DHH's selfish actions is the dramatic moment of Marcus's epiphany regarding his new ethnic identity, as it allows him entry into a whole new experience and culture. He discovers his ethnic voice when he is with a group of Asian college students, which is where DHH first publicly tries out his hoodwinking story about Marcus. With the students, Marcus finds a community of like-minded individuals, telling them: "Do you know how special this is? Out there—in the rest of America—everyone's on their own, fighting to stay afloat. But *you*—you've got each other. No, *we've* got each other!" (32). Marcus's willing embrace of Asian and Asian American culture and the students' reflective embrace of him finally provides him with an authentic sense of identity and connection. There is a comfort within the community and a personal awakening, as Teresa Botelho noted: "Marcus refashions himself and becomes what he feels he is."[13] Ironically, DHH bestows upon Marcus an Asian community that is missing from DHH's life. The end of the first act ends triumphantly with Marcus playing the King in *The King and I*, one of the most notorious examples of yellowface in the theater. In this case, though, DHH made possible Marcus's ascension as one of the first (assumed) Asian Americans to play the role.

The second act is much darker as it moves from the comedic situation of DHH and Marcus's ethnic identity to the actual race baiting that occurred in the 1990s as the government and press, represented by a character named NWOAOC (Name Withheld on Advice of Counsel), questioned Chinese Americans' honesty and allegiance to the country. Hwang uses actual examples of persecution, including that of Wen Ho Lee, an engineer at Los Alamos, who was accused of spying by the federal government but was never brought to trial (most of the espionage charges against him were dropped, and he accepted a guilty plea on one minor charge). In addition, HYH is dragged into the fray as questions arise about Chinese money that passed through his bank, money that may have been used to influence the Clinton re-election campaign. Unlike some who might be afraid at having to testify before Congress, HYH looks forward to receiving a subpoena because his presence in the halls of Congress only proves how great a country the United States is—that it would allow an immigrant to speak before a congressional committee. DHH eventually receives a visit from NWOAOC, who has reported most of the negative stories against Chinese Americans. From the early part of the interview it is clear the reporter has his own bias against Chinese Americans, and he continues to investigate HYH, even though he has already been cleared by the government.

NWOAOC: Well, now, they're reopening the case. Mr. Hwang, your father is a Chinese banker.
DHH: Chinese American.
NWOAOC: Exactly.
DHH: There's a difference. (60)

DHH confronts the racist attacks and suspicions in this extended scene between the reporter and himself, and DHH finally throws aside his own selfish concerns to defend his father against the accusations by the newspaper. Although the reporter manages to frighten DHH with his accusations, DHH eventually catches the reporter in a biased statement when he asks the reason behind his pressure on and distrust of Chinese Americans.

NWOAOC: Because there's no conflict between being white and being American.
DHH: Did you really just say that? There's a conflict—between being Chinese and being American? (61)

NWOAOC's misspoken words about Chinese Americans highlight the same issue that Hwang has expressed over the years—the complexity surrounding American identity for Asian Americans, arising from the reality that when non-Asians see an Asian face, they assume the person comes from another country and therefore cannot be a true citizen of the United States. After all, the thinking goes, an Asian face is not an American face. Hwang argues that such prejudices create a situation where being Chinese in America is akin to being a permanent foreigner. Hwang remarked: "You can have been in the country for several generations and people still go, 'Oh you speak really good English'. Basically this can be just irritating or it can be dangerous, in terms of for instance the internment of Japanese Americans during WWII, or the fact that whenever there are trade differences or the tension ratchets up between the US and Asian countries nowadays, there is a corresponding increase in anti-Asian violence in the States."[14] *Yellow Face* allows Hwang to show the injustice of a prejudice based only on the face of an individual that is then generalized to an entire population. NWOAOC thinks that someone who is Chinese cannot be true to America, but the play debunks NWOAOC's notion through HYH, who was born in China and yet even while in China felt a kinship with the United States. HYH tells his son: "When I was a kid in Shanghai, my favorite star of all was Jimmy Stewart. He was so kind, always doing things for other people. And when the chips were down, he would give it to the bad guys, tell them off, and everyone would listen to him. When I started the bank, I thought, Now, I can be Jimmy Stewart, too" (64). HYH's life story proves that a personal and emotional connection can and does occur between Asians and America.

In addition, Hwang provides a counterexample through Marcus, who is at the center of a continuing subplot about his journey to China. He has traveled to the East to connect with his adopted country, and during his stay, he finds himself taken with the Dong, an ethnic minority found mostly in southern China, and the song that the entire village sings. At first he is just an outsider, watching and listening as the villagers sing, but in his last missive to DHH, he relays an event at which he was invited into the villagers' circle and cajoled to sing with them, to join in their community song. Through this inclusion of an American by the inhabitants of a remote Chinese village, the play ends by asking this question: if the suspicions among Chinese villagers about an outsider can be washed away, then why cannot the United States embrace an ethnic group that has been in the country for more than 150 years? *Yellow Face* posits that while Asian Americans have come much further in recent decades, the journey is not yet complete. DHH looks forward to a time when he can "take words like 'Asian' and 'American,' like 'race' and 'nation,' mess them up so bad no one has any idea what they even mean anymore" (68–69). As Hwang has argued through his plays for thirty years, the external self and the internal self are two completely different entities. Marcus has learned that lesson and found his authentic self through his engagement with and acceptance by both the Asian American community and the Dong in China. DHH, despite all his plays to the contrary, still finds himself at the conclusion of *Yellow Face,* sitting alone on the stage, alienated from his ethnic community because of his narrow perspective about identity and still trying to balance his external face with what he wants to be on the inside.

Chinglish

As the most successful Chinese American artist on Broadway, Hwang became a sought-after consultant by various Chinese governmental agencies wanting to develop their own theatrical productions for Broadway. In the mid-2000s Hwang found himself travelling to China numerous times for developmental meetings. Ironically, *M. Butterfly,* which made Hwang the Broadway success so attractive to the Chinese, was still a banned work in China. While at Stanford, Hwang took a few courses in Chinese but not enough to speak the language, so during his visits he relied on interpreters and their varied levels of skills in English. The tenuous nature of communicating through translation was foregrounded when he visited a newly built theater, which featured "gorgeous Brazilian wood, Italian marble, [and] state-of-the-art Japanese sound systems."[15] Despite the quality of the construction, the signs in the facility were horribly mistranslated into English, and one sign identified a bathroom for the handicapped as the "Deformed Man's Toilet." In 2010, when Hwang and production team members for *Chinglish* went to China, they attended a banquet where they were served "wood frog fallopian tubes."[16] It turned out they were eating some type of edible fungus. He encountered numerous mistranslations like these during his trips to China. According to linguists, these problematic (and at times comical) translations stem from a belief that all languages share the same wording, so that one can substitute words freely from one language to another and create comprehensible sentences. With *Chinglish* Hwang aimed to address this problem of cultural miscommunication by highlighting how the United States and China fail to recognize the difficult nature of communication at its most basic level. If these two countries cannot communicate clearly about the most basic needs (toilets and food), then how can individuals from each country engage in the much more heady negotiations required in the public world of business and in the emotional and private intimacy of romance?

Because of his numerous visits to China and his increasing awareness of Chinglish, of which the mistranslations in the preceding paragraph are examples, Hwang decided to write about the communication problems faced by an American businessman trying to do business in China, where he does not speak the language and finds a different set of values and beliefs about the nature of business and private relationships. At the heart of the play's cultural confusion is a term called *guanxi,* which is central to relations in China.

The Goodman Theatre's *Playbill* included short essays about China to help the audience with the various cultural elements that figure in the play, including *guanxi:* "*Guanxi* is often considered more crucial to business than signed contracts—especially since the concept actually predates China's written language. Like much that defines the nation's culture, *guanxi* was essentially codified by Confucius, who defined the social order as a matter of people knowing their place: juniors respecting their seniors, seniors likewise owing their juniors benevolence. What is key to this principle is that exchange works both ways, and any relationship beyond family or institutional relationships involves a more elaborate, less tangible system of accounting."[17] The different cultural codes that prevail in Chinese business relations were not the only focus of the play. Hwang was also interested in the identity issues inherent in being an ethnic minority, as personified by the British character Peter, who has lived in China for more than a decade and still struggles to find acceptance from the people with whom he interacts every day.[18] Hwang experienced that same disconnect as an Asian in a country whose majority is Caucasian. However, as he traveled around the world, he realized that "this sense of dislocation and insecurity about identity applies to a lot of people. And I think Peter was an opportunity for me to explore these sorts of feelings of identity confusion but with the shoe on the other foot. Having spent some time with the ex-pat community in China, I would say it is more difficult for someone like Peter to be accepted as a Chinese person in China than it is for a Chinese American to be accepted as an American."[19]

Chinglish represented a major shift in the direction of Hwang's writing, as he pursued an international perspective on the ways of the world. When it comes to theater in the twenty-first century, he argued, "Our theater and our popular culture and our stories should resonate on an international level and we should be aware of what's going on in the rest of the world."[20] While *Yellow Face* allowed Hwang to provide a summing up of multiculturalism, which was a primary focus of his first thirty years as a playwright, *Chinglish* was his first focused foray into the world of internationalism. While some may argue that *M. Butterfly* introduced some elements of internationalism, it was not the play's main focus. Hwang explained the reason for his change in theatrical direction: "I'm less interested in the Asian-American thing at the moment. Thirty years ago when we were talking about Asian-American identity, identity politics, that was all fresh and exciting. And now it's like, we've already done that. And I am not that interested in it anymore."[21] In addition, the play provided him an opportunity to explore American's changing view toward the Chinese, noting that "over the course of just my little lifetime, the image of China in this country has gone 180 degrees. I remember when Chinese people were sort of seen as poor, uneducated menial laborers: cooks, waiters, laundrymen. And now Chinese are seen as having too much money, too much power and raise the curve in your math class."[22] Finally, *Chinglish* was the first he had written that featured the business world as the primary background. For this new area of interest he drew inspiration from David Mamet's *Glengarry Glen Ross,* with its focus on the cutthroat nature of sales and the games played by businessmen.

Of all of Hwang's plays, *Chinglish* was the most demanding when it came to casting its actors. The Chinese characters required performers who could speak English and also were fluent in Mandarin, reinforcing the complexity of the thematic element of cross-cultural communication. Hwang intended to give his Chinese characters the dignity of their own language, rather than having them speak English. Even more demanding was the fact that the actor playing the character Peter Timms had to speak English with a convincing English accent and also be fluent in Mandarin.[23] In Hwang's play, 25 percent of the dialogue was in Chinese. The use of Mandarin placed Hwang's non-Mandarin-speaking audience in a position similar to that of Daniel, the American businessman and the only character in the play who speaks no Mandarin. The audience can empathize with his inability to follow the conversations, but, unlike Daniel, the audience does have the benefit of the supertitles and because of them can appreciate the humor when the translators mistranslate what has been said. Hwang remarked on the inherent theatrical benefits of the supertitles, which mirrored his experience in opera. "It seems like audiences really respond to and embrace the titles, to some extent, because the titles provide a lot of the comedy, and there's something satisfying about the fact that the audience knows what everybody on stage is saying even though the characters may not be able to understand each other."[24]

After finishing the first draft in January 2010 and eliciting immediate interest from producers, Hwang wanted to see the level of audience interest in the subject matter of his latest play. He knew that if the play opened in California (where his last three New York–bound plays had opened), it would have no problem finding an audience as it would appeal to the state's Asian American populace. Hwang, though, wondered whether his new work would be of interest to a middle-American audience, and for that reason *Chinglish* had its world premiere in Chicago at the Goodman Theatre in June 2011. On the basis of the play's commercial and artistic success in Chicago, where it extended its initial run, as well as the producers' belief that audiences were ready for the Chinese–American subject matter, especially since it was couched in Hwang's comedic writing style, it was decided that the play would move directly to Broadway, making it Hwang's third Broadway play. It opened on October 27, 2011.

It is not surprising that the reviews from Chicago helped convince the producers that the play could succeed on Broadway. The *Chicago Tribune* heralded *Chinglish* as the best play Hwang had written since *M. Butterfly*. Chris Jones of the *Tribune* said that the only element missing was a "willingness to confront the play's darker themes and add to the quotient of bicultural shivers," while Mary Houlihan of the *Chicago Sun-Times* found that even though the play revolves around the "one-joke comedy" of translation confusions, Hwang "uncovers a bit of the soul of modern China." The reviews from New York were not so ebullient. Marilyn Stasio of *Variety* was positive in her reaction to the play, remarking that "this well-made comedy takes a poignant view of the profound isolation and terrible vulnerability of people who are lost without their native language." However, this concept was lost because of the size of the theater. She suggested that *Chinglish* would be better served in a smaller venue. Ben Brantley of the *New York Times* called the play "sporadically funny" when "English is merrily mutilated" but found that the play was not very deep, as it was "laid out with the frame-by-frame exactness of a comic strip." He also felt that the characters "are about as personally involving as the brightly colored, illustrative figures in a PowerPoint presentation" because Hwang relied on "quick-stroke portraits" similar to what one might find in "satiric sketch comedy" rather than providing any depth. The one exception to his criticism was the character Xi, Daniel's love interest, who he thought was finely drawn. Ultimately, "this play feels too solidly grounded for its own good." Hilton Als, writing in *The New Yorker*, also noted that the play was composed of short scenes, which gave it the feel of a sitcom. In addition, "Hwang's characters have quirks, rather than characteristics, and you don't take much away from the play that you haven't already read in the newspapers. It's journalism theatre: flat, effective, and to the point." Finally, Terry Teachout of the *Wall Street Journal* had a mixed reaction to the play. He wrote: "The second act is deeper in tone, enough so that you wish the first act had taken more chances. But Mr. Hwang wrings the most out of his one joke, and the results, if slight, are thoroughly satisfying."[25] *Chinglish*'s run on Broadway was much shorter than anticipated, lasting only 109 performances. The play had cost $3.5 million dollars to produce. It received three Drama Desk nominations, including one for best play and one for Jennifer Lim, who played Xi. Despite the early Tony buzz surrounding Jennifer Lim's performance as Xi, the play received no Tony nominations. However, the play was optioned to be made into a Hollywood feature film with Hwang slated to write the screenplay adaptation.

Like *FOB,* which opens with a lecture by Dale to the audience about the nature of FOBs, *Chinglish* opens with a PowerPoint presentation by Daniel, a businessman who has worked in China, to Ohio businessmen to help them navigate the complicated Chinese governmental structure for finalizing contracts. The play then flashes back three years to Daniel's first trip to China, when he sought to convince government officials in Guiyang to hire his sign-making company for their city's new cultural center. In order to navigate the system, Daniel hires Peter, who has been in China for more than a decade and speaks fluent Mandarin, to help him make his way through the process. He quickly learns that what he thought would be a one-week visit will actually require an eight-week stay, as Chinese rely on relationships to close business deals. During the course of his stay, he comes to learn from Xi, the vice minister of culture, that he will never get the contract for making the center's signs because Cai, the cultural minister overseeing the task, has already promised the contract to a family member. Xi, though, offers to secretly help him break the impasse, which eventually requires Daniel to let Peter go. As Daniel and Xi work together, they begin an affair. During one of their trysts, Xi learns that Daniel has lied about the financial health of his company. However, she changes her mind about abandoning Daniel when he reveals that he previously worked for Enron and was employed there during the company's collapse. Ironically, his involvement with the financial disaster makes him a much more attractive business partner because of his previous professional relationship with the internationally recognized figures who caused the economic scandal. Their involvement with Daniel allows her city to be one step removed from economic greatness, thus raising the city's stature. The government agrees with Xi and hires Daniel, having discovered Cai's nepotism and imprisoned him. After the victory Daniel thinks he and Xi should ditch their spouses and become a couple, but he learns that Xi's reason for helping him win his contract was to help her husband move up in the government. Daniel, though, ends up with the contract, which leads to many more, saving his family business and turning him into an expert in Chinese–American business dealings.

While Daniel tries to remake his identity after the failure at Enron and to become the savior of his family's business, Hwang focuses his play not only on the Chinese world of business but also, and more important, on the nature of communication when it comes to business dealings (and, later, romantic dealings) and the inherent difficulties in translating the languages of the most important economic powers of the world and the words of their representatives. The existence of such communication problems are established through Daniel's opening presentation about Chinese signs that have been poorly translated into English. These kind of signs prompted Daniel's journey to China, where he tries to promote himself as a manufacturer who can produce correctly translated signs, so that Guiyang can save face with its English-speaking guests. When Daniel first meets with the city officials with his proposal, he points out, almost gleefully, the numerous examples of embarrassing signs at the Pudong Grand Theatre in Shanghai. However, his American hubris, which leads him to point out errors made by Chinese translators, gets Daniel into trouble with Xi, who reminds Daniel that the misuse of other countries' languages does not just occur in her country. English-speaking countries are as guilty of misusing Chinese as the Chinese are of misusing English. She produces a copy of a scientific journal by the Max Planck Institute with Chinese characters on the cover. The scientific editors believed they were printing a Chinese poem, but instead the characters on the cover are actually sexual come-ons. It appears, according to Xi, that the editors "pulled some ad off a girlie bar in Shanghai!"[26] And yet, despite the mistaken interpretations of each other's language, Xi and Daniel do find that at a primal level China and the United States share a few common terms. This comes up when, at a dinner, Xi tells Daniel that Cai has already promised the contract to his sister-in-law.

DANIEL: Right, right. So am I just—screwed?
(*Xi laughs.*)
XI: [In Chinese] Dirty old man.
DANIEL: Oh, that? That you know? You know "screwed"?
XI: All person know "screwed"! (46–47)

The next example of problematic communication occurs with the translators. When Daniel meets with the city officials, Peter translates for him. The government officials rely on an employee to translate their Chinese into English for Daniel. While Peter's Mandarin is exquisite, drawing numerous compliments in meetings, the English of the Chinese translators (three appear over the course of the play) is woefully inadequate. They continually struggle and flub words, highlighting the fact that the signs are merely one facet of the communication problem between the two countries, since clear and direct communication does not occur even in face-to-face meetings. In the first meeting Qian mangles Daniel's words of introduction. Daniel introduces his company by saying, "We're a small family firm," which Qian translates as "His company is tiny and insignificant" (12). Later Daniel begins his pitch by saying, "And here is why we're worth the money." Qian renders his words as "He will explain why he spends money so recklessly" (20). While the mistakes are extremely humorous theatrically, in a business sense they are deadly. Luckily for Daniel, Peter corrects Qian's ongoing misstatements. Her incompetency, however, extends beyond translation when Peter and Cai begin to discuss their passion for a specific Chinese opera. Qian is not familiar with it and is unable to explain to Daniel the nature of the discussion taking place. As Cai complains about the lack of cultural knowledge among Chinese youth, Qian turns to Daniel, explaining, "They are discussing my ignorance" (27), which is almost the only thing she accurately translates. By the end of the scene the importance of communication is highlighted by Xi's demand that Qian be fired. At a later meeting Qian has been replaced by Bing, the nephew of Cai, but his translation of Chinese into English is as problematic as Qian's. He translates Chinese only into sexually provocative English phrases. When Cai explains that he is unable to offer Daniel the contract by saying "My hands are tied," Bing translates the sentence as "He is in bondage" (67). Later, Cai speaks to Peter about his inability to make the deal happen, telling him, "Teacher Peter, I cannot approve this proposal," which becomes "He cannot fulfill your desires" (67–68). While Daniel may have felt some sympathy for Qian, he recognizes just how inept Bing is and tells Peter that the new translator is worse than the previous one. The final meeting, as Daniel moves up the government chain of command, includes a third translator, Zhao, who is better than the other two but who struggles with colloquialisms. When Daniel explains his position with the company as "I recently assumed control of Ohio Signage and now direct all its operations," Zhao manages to get half of the phrasing right, telling the Chinese delegation, "Mr. Cavenaugh now controls Ohio Signage and . . . and he is also a surgeon" (92–93). Because of the presence of Peter and, later, Xi, who speaks some English learned during her days as a foreign exchange student in Sri Lanka, Daniel manages to survive the meetings with his talking points intact, but, as he tells his assembled audience in Ohio, "When doing business in China, always bring your own translator" (8).

However, these issues of mistranslation can be righted by having qualified translators, like Peter, just as the linguistic errors on the signs can eventually be corrected. However, a third instance of cultural miscommunication and misunderstanding occurs in Daniel's face-to-face interactions with the Chinese officials. The translation issues are secondary to the more problematic nature of how people from China and people from the United States, which have starkly different cultural practices, interact and develop trust in each other if they do not comprehend and appreciate the subtler aspects of the different cultures. When Peter and Daniel first meet, Peter instructs Daniel in the concept of *guanxi,* which differentiates Chinese business practices from the usual Western way of doing business. He tells Daniel that it all comes down to "Relationships. It's almost a cliché now, but business in China is built on relationships" (9). Because of the weakness of the Chinese judicial system in maintaining the legal obligations of contracts, business revolves around the importance of relationships, which take precedence over any other form of agreement or negotiating tool. A Chinese business partner might indicate that a contract will be bestowed on a Western company, but if there is no *guanxi* between the two individuals, then there is no real contract. Peter instructs Daniel that "The trick is to understand that all these outcomes take place *outside* the formal justice system" (9). Because of *guanxi* Daniel's trip extends from a week to eight weeks to ensure that he develops the proper rapport with his government contacts.

Peter believes that he has established *guanxi* with Cai because he tutored Cai's intellectually challenged son and succeeded in getting him into an English university. For this act of friendship and assistance, Peter knows that, because of the rules of *guanxi,* Cai must reciprocate. Believing he has an inroad, he turns himself into a contractor who can help Western businessmen who come to China. The problem is that while Peter understands the tit-for-tat aspect of *guanxi,* he struggles to find his way into the private and personal realm of relationships. After all, the cultural minister's bond with his sister-in-law trumps any obligation he feels toward Peter, because family relations supersede all others. Feeling betrayed, Peter berates Cai at a business meeting for not holding true to the rules of *guanxi* when, in fact, Peter does not understand the rules well enough. Because of Peter's explosion as well as Xi's decision to help Daniel get the contract, Daniel cannot keep Peter, who has lost face because of his outburst; keeping Peter in his employ would reflect negatively on Daniel.

Daniel's path to achieving *guanxi* is not a smooth one. His problem hinges on the fact that, over the course of many meetings, he does not reveal the entire truth about his company, which is in dire financial distress, and about his past, which is tainted by his association with Enron. In fact, he believes that because he does not speak Chinese, he can more easily hide his past from the government officials, once again suggesting the Western businessman's hubris and his belief in his ability to fool his Eastern counterparts, who are new to the Western style of business. He tells Xi, who accidentally discovers his lies: "No one at home will touch me! But I thought—maybe if I went all the way to China, steered clear of the big cities—maybe I could pull this off. Take the ruined shell of my family firm. Land a deal. And become someone new. Someplace far away, where hardly anyone can understand a word I'm saying" (82). Ironically, for someone who argues for clarity in communication as he pushes for the contract to make the signs for the cultural center, Daniel believes that the same communication difficulties will be a boon for him and his company, allowing him to hide his dire situation behind the confusion of language and cultural differences. However, Daniel quickly learns that his expectation that the East will reject him because of his past indiscretions is completely wrong. Once again, in Hwang's world, a Westerner misreads his Eastern counterparts. Xi reacts excitedly to Daniel's Enron connection, seeing it as a positive rather than a negative. She makes his involvement with Enron the selling point for Guiyang officials, as they marvel in hushed deference at his relationships with Enron's dethroned masters of the universe, Kenneth Lay and Jeffrey Skilling. The company's failure is not as important as Daniel's stature in the company, the relationship he had with the swindlers, and the international reputation of the company. Dealing with a businessman of his prominence raises the importance of Guiyang, which considers itself to be of little value in China, despite its population of four million. Enron's corruption is not critical to these officials, since, as Peter explained, the justice system in China is absent. Relationships are more important, and Daniel's past association with Enron makes him a valuable business partner. Daniel discovers, much to his surprise, that what is considered a liability in the United States is an advantage in China. As Daniel says near the end of the play: "There I was, thinking I had to lie about my past. Cover it up. But you knew, I could tell the truth. And everything would be OK. Better than OK. That by telling the truth. I got the deal. Got my Guanxi" (107).

While Daniel eventually does achieve *guanxi* in terms of his contract with the city, he fails in attaining *guanxi* with Xi because he misreads the meaning of the term outside the world of business. Since Daniel and Xi are lovers, he correctly views their lovemaking as a form of *guanxi*, as she wants to help him win the contracts. However, Daniel conflates *guanxi* with love by misreading her comments about her husband as a suggestion that they could be something more than surreptitious lovers. Both partners are in marriages that are troubled. Xi tells Daniel of her disappointment in her husband, a local judge, who she thinks is selfish and uncommunicative.

DANIEL: You don't love your husband?
XI: Once—long time—but, no. Today, only husband.

DANIEL: Then why don't you . . . you know, break up? Escape your
  marriage?
XI: Yes, escape. But. Not so easy.
DANIEL: You mean, here. In China. Marriage is hard to—?
XI: Not so easy. (65)

On the basis of her comments, Daniel believes that their romantic attachment
could become more. Since both of them are unhappy with their spouses,
why should they stay married to them? Daniel proposes that they should be
together. However, Daniel's Western notion of love does not translate into
the culture of China. When he presses the point with Xi, he finds out that
she has a very different concept about the direction of their relationship. For
Xi, her sexual relationship with Daniel allows her to escape from the routine
and drudgery of marriage, which she calls "the death" (109). However, escape is all that their lovemaking provides for her. When Daniel explains that
he views their relationship as one defined by love, Xi dismisses his words as
being too American, noting: "'Love,' it is your American religion" (110). For
Xi her relationship with her husband is not about love; instead, they share
a much more complex notion called *qíng yì,* which defies easy translation
into English.

XI: Qíng yì. Marriage: Qíng yì.
DANIEL: And what does that mean?
XI: Qíng yì is like comrade. (110)

Unlike all the other Chinese terms that Daniel has encountered, whether the
mistranslated bathroom signs or the conversations in the business meetings
or *guanxi, qíng yì* is the first Chinese term that cannot be translated into
English, a fact that contradicts his business contention that all Chinese can
be translated into acceptable, understandable English. At the heart of *qíng
yì* is the concept that Chinese marriage is not based on love, unlike American marriages, which stereotypically make love the defining building block
of the relationship. However, Hwang explained that "not just Chinese but
people in old-world cultures in general view marriage as an institution, with
the understanding that romantic love fades."[27] Love is a concept associated
with long-term Western relationships. Love does not linger as long in China.

Xi reveals that she and her husband did have a romantic and passionate
start to their relationship, but now they have moved on to another level that
links them. They are bound by a commitment and a sense of obligation that
go beyond romantic love. They are now comrades, as she says, or perhaps,

in an American sense, they are the sole teammates on a two-person team, and, while they may no longer really like each other, they are bound by the nature of their loyalty and honor to support each other. For Daniel, then, his relationship with Xi is predicated on the premise that she no longer has any need or connection to her husband, just as he has little need for his wife. In contrast, while Xi's sexual relationship with Daniel provides her an escape and is done completely for her own enjoyment, Xi's business deal with Daniel is a deliberate scheme to help her husband achieve a higher position in the city through the removal of Cai from office, on the grounds that he was moving too slowly on economic reforms for the city. With Cai imprisoned, Xi's husband, who ended up approving Daniel's contract for the signs, will move up in the city's hierarchy. In both respects, Xi's interest in Daniel is not an investment in him at all but instead an investment in her own sexual needs, her husband's promotion, and a better system of government for her city. Daniel's self-interested, personal perspective, a distinctly American take on their relationship, falls victim to Xi's more practical and community-based Eastern philosophy. While both Daniel and Xi are successful, the difference between them is palpable in terms of what is gained. Daniel's small company is saved to do more business with the Chinese, but Xi's actions have a much larger ripple effect throughout her city. Their values are strikingly different and perhaps suggest the changing power relationship between the two countries that Daniel tries to make clear to Xi.

XI: One day, China will be strong!
(*She grabs her overcoat.*)
DANIEL: Wait. What are you—? "One day"? You're strong now!
   We're the ones who are weak!
(*Pause.*)
XI: What?
DANIEL: China—strong! America—weak!
XI: Some day.
DANIEL: No. Now! (78–79)

Daniel sees what Xi and her colleagues still do not. China's way of business, while startlingly different from the West's, is improving the country's position and power in the world.

   As in M. *Butterfly,* Hwang presents a character who has misread the East. Unlike Gallimard in M. *Butterfly,* though, Daniel learns from his mistakes and comes away from the experience an educated and successful man. As Hwang has done throughout his plays, he shows the importance of balance in helping people succeed when bridging two cultures. Daniel is Hwang's first Caucasian character to learn that lesson as he embraces the Chinese way of business to regain prosperity in the Western world, succeeding where others have failed.

A Coda

After *Chinglish* opened, Hwang received comments from Chinese audience members who pointed out one unbelievable element in his play: the fact that a high-ranking Chinese government official's wife would have an affair with a Western businessman. They corrected him, according to Hwang, saying that it "might make for good drama, but couldn't actually happen in China. Such a woman would never enter into a close relationship with a foreign man."[28] However, shortly after the play closed, the Chinese government began to ask questions about the suspicious death of Neil Heywood, an English businessman, and his is-it-more-than-just-business relationship with Gu Kailai, the wife of Bo Xilai, a party leader who was picked to ascend rapidly through the top governmental ranks. Hwang suddenly found *Chinglish* back in the news as newspaper reporters and Chinese experts began sending him headline-type missives that connected his play with the suspicious death: "*Chinglish* à la Agatha Christie!" and "*Chinglish* as a murder mystery!"[29] The controversy became the focus of international news stories in the winter and spring of 2012, and *Newsweek* asked Hwang to offer his own prognostication on the outcome of the political and criminal scandal. He wrote: "Still, it's unlikely we'll ever learn the true facts of this case. For Chinese officials, obsessed with 'face,' the real scandal is that ordinary Chinese, even foreigners, have seen the inner workings of the nation's ruling elite. *Chinglish* uses power struggles, plot twists, and translated supertitles to make transparent what is normally hidden to outsiders. In the real China, though truth may be as strange as fiction, it is almost always less transparent."[30] And yet, despite Hwang's prediction of obfuscation, in August 2012 China revealed to the international press that Gu Kailai had been tried and found guilty of murdering Heywood, who had threatened to reveal information about shady business dealings. Clearly, to judge just from this case, the nature of China and its changing relationships within its own borders and with the West are still works in progress.

China, Asian Americans, and the United States have experienced dramatic changes with regard to culture, gender, politics, and economics over the past thirty years, and Hwang has documented those effects not only on China and Asian Americans but also on Americans as a whole. With his professed new focus on internationalization in his plays, Hwang opens up vast new possibilities to explore as the world's people grow closer. As the case of Heywood's murder attests, the divide between East and West is smaller than it ever has been before, providing a treasure trove of rich material. No doubt, in future works, Hwang, with his keen eye for examining our lives, will revel in exploring the constantly evolving notions of ethnicity, citizenship, and, most important, identity in both the East and the West.

NOTES

Chapter 1—Understanding David Henry Hwang

1. Jeremy Gerard, "David Hwang: Riding on the Hyphen," *New York Times Magazine,* 13 March 1988.

2. Lyons, "'Making His Muscles Work,'" 236.

3. Moss-Coane, "David Henry Hwang," 284.

4. Gerard, "David Hwang."

5. Moss-Coane, "David Henry Hwang," 285.

6. David Henry Hwang, "A New Musical by Rodgers and Hwang," *New York Times,* 13 October 2002.

7. Ibid.

8. Ibid.

9. David Phair, "You Don't Need Most of the Stuff You Learn," *South China Morning Post,* 1 July 2006: EDUCATION 5.

10. Ibid.

11. Hwang, "Worlds Apart," 50.

12. Savran, "David Hwang," 119.

13. Lyons, "'Making His Muscles Work,'" 237.

14. John Beer, "Playwright David Henry Hwang," *Time Out Chicago,* 20 June 2011.

15. Lyons, "'Making His Muscles Work,'" 240.

16. Dinitia Smith, "Face Values: The Sexual and Racial Obsessions of David Henry Hwang," *New York,* 11 January 1993: 43.

17. Ruth Leon, "One Fine Play We Will See," *Times* (London), 17 March 1989.

18. Smith, "Face Values," 43.

19. Lyons, "'Making His Muscles Work,'" 241.

20. Savran, "David Hwang," 119.

21. Ibid., 120.

22. Dennis Polkow, "Chinglish Lessons: The Playwright on the Chicago Summer of David Hwang," *New City Stage,* 15 June 2011.

23. David Henry Hwang, e-mail message to author, 14 August 2012.

24. Lyons, "'Making His Muscles Work,'" 236.

25. Savran, "David Hwang," 123.

26. Bryer, "David Henry Hwang," 133.

27. Gerard, "David Hwang."

28. Ibid.

29. Jack Viertel, "Fun with Race and the Media," *American Theatre*, April 2008: 61. *EBSCO*.

30. Hwang, "Response," 224.

31. Chapter 4 features a look at some of the disgruntled reactions of Asian American scholars to Hwang and his representation of Asians in *M. Butterfly*.

32. Kim, *Asian American Theatre*, 136.

Chapter 2—Hwang's Asian American Trilogy

1. Lyons, "'Making His Muscles Work,'" 238.

2. Phair, "You Don't Need."

3. Bruce Weber, "A Family's Tales of China as a Path to Theatre Fame," *New York Times*, 30 March 1998: E1.

4. Joe Brown, "On Wings of a *Butterfly*: Playwright David Henry Hwang, Broadway Bound," *Washington Post*, 10 February 1988: B1.

5. Weber, "A Family's Tales."

6. Gerard, "David Hwang."

7. Ibid.

8. Esther Lee Kim explored why David Henry Hwang and *FOB* became of such interest to Joseph Papp and the Public Theater. Part of Kim's argument stemmed from the rapidity of Hwang's ascension as the leading Asian American playwright without having ever been vetted through any of the established Asian American theatre groups. While she acknowledged that part of the success can be attributed to Hwang's writing talent as well as the artistic excellence of John Lone, who played Steve, and Mako, the play's director, she posited that Hwang's rise coincided with an affirmative action policy that was in place at the Public Theater, thus allowing for his numerous productions. See Kim, *Asian American Theatre*, 129–37.

9. Savran, "David Hwang," 123.

10. Quoted reviews in this paragraph come from the following sources, listed respectively: Anonymous, review of *FOB*, *Christian Science Monitor*, 12 June 1980: 18; and Frank Rich, "*FOB* Rites of Immigrant Passage," *New York Times*, 10 June 1980: C6.

11. Gerard, "David Hwang."

12. Savran, "David Hwang," 120.

13. Ibid.

14. Jew, "Dismantling the Realist Character," 197.

15. Cooperman, "Boundaries of Cultural Identity," 366.

16. Cooperman, "New Theatrical Statements," 204–5.

17. Hwang, *FOB*, *Trying to Find Chinatown*, 31. Subsequent page references appear in the text.

18. Wang, "Reimagining Political Community," 266.

19. Jew, "Dismantling the Realist Character," 199–200.

20. Dong, "Mulan against Gwan Gung," 109.

21. Jew, "Dismantling the Realist Character," 201.

22. Rabkin, "The Sound of a Voice," 100.

23. Moy, *Marginal Sights*, 126.

24. Dong, "Mulan against Gwan Gung," 106.

25. Wang, "Reimagining Political Community," 265.

26. Eric Pace, "I Write Plays to Claim a Place for Asian-Americans," *New York Times*, 12 July 1981: sec. 2:4.

27. Selim, "The Theatre of David Henry Hwang," 117.

28. Pace, "I Write Plays."

29. Cooperman, "New Theatrical Statements," 205.

30. Savran, "David Hwang," 129.

31. Quoted reviews in this paragraph come from the following sources, listed respectively: John Beaufort, "GBS Rail Strike," *Christian Science Monitor*, 27 July 1981: 15; and Frank Rich, review of *The Dance and the Railroad*, New York Times, 31 March 1981: C5.

32. Hwang, *The Dance and the Railroad, Trying to Find Chinatown*, 66. Subsequent page references appear in the text.

33. Wang, "Reimagining Political Community," 268.

34. Ibid., 269.

35. Dickey, "'Myths of the East, Myths of the West,'" 275.

36. Cooperman, "New Theatrical Statements," 206.

37. Savran, "David Hwang," 125–26.

38. Gerard, "David Hwang."

39. Cooperman, "New Theatrical Statements," 208.

40. Gerard, "David Hwang."

41. Bryer, "David Henry Hwang," 133.

42. Lyons, "'Making His Muscles Work,'" 236.

43. Street, *David Henry Hwang*, 28.

44. Quoted reviews in this paragraph come from the following sources, listed respectively: John Beaufort, "Satiric Drama," *Christian Science Monitor*, 27 October 1981: 19; Frank Rich, review of *Family Devotions*, *New York Times*, 19 October 1981: C17; and Edith Oliver, review of *Family Devotions*, *New Yorker*, 2 November 1981: 65.

45. Hwang, *Family Devotions, Trying to Find Chinatown*, 119. Subsequent page references appear in the text.

Chapter 3 — Two Experiments

1. Hwang, "David Henry Hwang," 93.

2. Cooperman, "Boundaries of Cultural Identity," 371.

3. Ibid., 370.

4. Hwang, "David Henry Hwang," 93.

5. Woo, "Gender Trouble," 302.

6. Street, *David Henry Hwang*, 32.

7. Cooperman, "New Theatrical Statements," 208.

8. Woo, "Gender Trouble," 307.

9. Don Shewey, "His Art Blends the Best of Two Cultures on Stage," *New York Times*, 30 October 1983.

10. Quoted reviews in this paragraph come from the following sources, listed respectively: John Simon, "Brotherhood Weak," *New York*, 21 November 1983: 66–67; and Frank Rich, review of *Sound and Beauty*, *New York Times*, 7 November 1983: C13.

11. Hwang, *The Sound of a Voice, Trying to Find Chinatown,* 156. Subsequent page references appear in the text.

12. Samuel Beckett, *Play, The Collected Shorter Plays* (New York: Grove, 1984), 156–57.

13. Hwang, "David Henry Hwang," 93.

14. Rabkin, "The Sound of a Voice," 108.

15. Ibid.

16. Woo, "Gender Trouble," 304.

17. Jew, "Gothic Aesthetics," 144.

18. Ibid., 145.

19. Ibid., 152.

20. Ibid., 147.

21. Hwang, *The House of Sleeping Beauties, Trying to Find Chinatown,* 184. Subsequent page references appear in the text.

22. Jew, "Gothic Aesthetics," 150.

23. Cooperman, "Boundaries of Cultural Identity," 369.

24. Ibid.

25. Savran, "David Hwang," 123.

26. Bryer, "David Henry Hwang," 131.

27. Moss-Coane, "David Henry Hwang," 283.

28. Quoted reviews in this paragraph come from the following sources, listed respectively: Frank Rich, "*Rich Relations,* from David Hwang," *New York Times,* 22 April 1986: C15; and Street, *David Henry Hwang,* 36, 39.

29. Hwang, *Rich Relations, FOB and Other Plays,* 226. Subsequent page references appear in the text.

Chapter 4—International Success

1. DiGaetani, "*M. Butterfly,*" 143.

2. Hwang, "Afterword," 96.

3. Ibid., 95.

4. The intertextual connections between *M. Butterfly* and its inspiration, Giacomo Puccini's *Madame Butterfly,* have been analyzed by a number of critics. See Kerr, "David Henry Hwang," 119–30; Ross, "On the Trail of the Butterfly," 111–22; and Jonathan Wisenthal, Sherrill Grace, and Melinda Boyd, eds., *A Vision of the Orient: Texts, Intertexts, and Contexts of* Madame Butterfly (Toronto: University of Toronto Press, 2006).

5. Rossini, "From *M. Butterfly* to *Bondage,*" 59.

6. Gerard, "David Hwang."

7. Ibid.

8. Kim, *Asian American Theatre,* 129.

9. Lee, "Between the Oriental and the Transvestite," 56.

10. Ibid.

11. Chang, "*M. Butterfly,*" 183.

12. Lin, "Staging Orientalia," 31.

13. Moy, *Marginal Sights,* 123.

14. Ibid., 125.

15. Ibid., 124.

16. Bryer, "David Henry Hwang," 143.

17. Ibid.

18. Cheng, "Race and Fantasy in Modern America," 180.

19. Bryer, "David Henry Hwang," 143.

20. Quoted reviews in this paragraph come from the following sources, listed respectively: Frank Rich, "*M. Butterfly,* A Story of a Strange Love, Conflict and Betrayal," *New York Times,* 21 March 1988: C13; John Gross, "A *Butterfly* That Hovers over the Issues of Racism, Sexism and Imperialism," *New York Times,* 10 April 1988: A47; John Beaufort, "Puccini Wouldn't Recognize It," *Christian Science Monitor,* 23 March 1988: 22; and Michael Feingold, "Transformational Glamour," *Village Voice,* 29 March 1988: 116.

21. Quoted reviews in this paragraph come from the following sources, listed respectively: Jacques Le Sourd, "*M. Butterfly,*" *USA Today,* 23 March 1988; Jack Kroll, "The Diplomat and the Diva," *Newsweek,* 4 April 1988; and John Simon, "Finding Your Song," *New York,* 11 April 1988: 117.

22. Since Hwang's play was the first Chinese American play to appear on Broadway, Angela Pao examined more than fifty reviews of *M. Butterfly* in order to dissect the mainstream reaction to such a watershed event. See Pao, "The Critic and the Butterfly," 1–16.

23. DiGaetani, "*M. Butterfly,*" 143.

24. Hwang, *M. Butterfly,* 11. Subsequent page references appear in the text.

25. Cheng, "Race and Fantasy in Modern America," 182.

26. Gerard, "David Hwang."

27. DiGaetani, "*M. Butterfly,*" 145.

28. Eng, "In the Shadows of a Diva," 142.

29. Space prohibits discussion of the topic, but the role of transvestism in *M. Butterfly* has been analyzed by a number of scholars, including John Bak, "*Vestis virum reddit:* The Gender Politics of Drag in Williams's *A Streetcar Named Desire* and Hwang's *M. Butterfly,*" *South Atlantic Review* (Fall 2005): 94–118; Garber, *Vested Interests,* 234–66; and Koh, "(Dis)Placing Identities," 246–54.

30. Kondo, *About Face,* 43.

31. Shin, "Projected Bodies," 188.

32. Lee, *Performing Asian America,* 112–13.

33. Ibid., 117.

34. Davis, "'Just a Man,'" 68.

35. Rossini, "From *M. Butterfly* to *Bondage,*" 60.

36. Grace, "Playing Butterfly," 149.

37. Hwang, "A Conversation with David Henry Hwang," 188.

Chapter 5 — After M. Butterfly

1. Why was there such an outcry over the protest and the ensuing decision? Hwang explained that "The atmosphere in the country around issues of race and culture were in a pressure cooker at that particular moment, and there was so much anger and so many feelings of resentment on all sides of the issue that were not being expressed—any opportunity to rally around an incident became a vent for everybody's pent-up frustrations on all sides of the issue." Viertel, "Fun with Race," 61.

2. Discussions of the *Miss Saigon* casting controversy can be found in Kim, *Asian American Theatre,* 183–92; Pao, "The Eyes of the Storm," 21–39; and Karen

Shimakawa, *National Abjections: The Asian American Body Onstage* (Durham, N.C.: Duke University Press, 2002), 43–53.

3. Misha Berson, "Playwright David Henry Hwang Won't Let Broadway Blues Get Him Down," *Seattle Times*, 19 April 1993.

4. Christine Dolen, "Kentucky's Drama Derby Yields Pack of Theatrical Thoroughbreds," *Miami Herald*, 29 March 1992;

5. Berson, "Playwright David Henry Hwang."

6. Bryer, "David Henry Hwang," 135.

7. Polkow, "Chinglish Lessons."

8. Ibid.

9. Ibid.

10. Dolen, "Kentucky's Drama Derby."

11. Bryer, "David Henry Hwang," 145.

12. Ibid.

13. Rossini, "From *M. Butterfly* to *Bondage*," 68.

14. Smith, "Face Values," 45.

15. Rossini, "From *M. Butterfly* to *Bondage*," 68.

16. Hwang, *Bondage, Trying to Find Chinatown*, 253. Subsequent page references appear in the text.

17. Tom Carter, "Playwright Hwang: 'I'm in a Very Productive Stage of My Life,'" *Lexington Herald-Leader*, 23 February 1992.

18. Frank Magiera, "Saving Face," *Worcester Telegram and Gazette*, 11 February 1993.

19. Iris Fanger, "Face Forward," *Boston Herald*, 5 February 1993.

20. Hwang, *Face Value*.

21. Fanger, "Face Forward."

22. Hwang, *Face Value*.

23. Quoted reviews in this paragraph come from the following sources, listed respectively: April Austin, "*Face Value* Takes On More Than It Can Deliver," *Christian Science Monitor*, 17 February 1993; Iris Fanger, "*Face Value* Falls Flat," *Boston Herald*, 15 February 1993; and Kevin Kelly, "Hwang's *Face Value* Flops on Its Farce," *Boston Globe*, 15 February 1993: 31.

24. Berson, "Playwright David Henry Hwang."

25. Berson, "The Demon," 50.

26. Berson, "Playwright David Henry Hwang."

27. Weber, "A Family's Tales."

28. Hwang, "Bringing Up *Child*," vi.

29. Steven Drukman, "Taking Bittersweet Journeys into the Past," *New York Times*, 10 November 1996: Sec 2:5.

30. Berson, "The Demon," 16.

31. Ibid.

32. Drukman, "Taking Bittersweet Journeys."

33. Lyons, "'Making His Muscles Work,'" 241.

34. Quoted reviews in this paragraph come from the following sources, listed respectively: Ben Brantley, "Extending a Hand to Ancestral Ghosts in China," *New York Times*, 20 November 1996: C20; and John Lahr, "Ghosts in the Machine," *New Yorker*, 2 December 1996: 123.

35. Hwang, "Bringing up *Child*," vii.

36. Ibid., ix.

37. Quoted reviews in this paragraph come from the following sources, listed respectively: Matt Wolf, "*Golden Child*," *Variety*, 3 April 1998; and Peter Marks, "The Unbinding of Traditions," *New York Times*, 3 April 1998: E1.

38. Hwang, *Golden Child*, 9. Subsequent page references appear in the text.

39. Berson "The Demon," 17.

40. Baines represented an inspired bit of writing by Hwang. Since Baines is a foreigner and does not speak Chinese, he communicates through pidgin Chinese. Hwang's depiction disrupts the stereotype of Chinese characters speaking pidgin English, placing awkward communication skills in the mouth of a Caucasian and, in turn, empowering the linguistic abilities of the Chinese characters.

41. Berson, "The Demon," 16.

Chapter 6—A Musical Hwang

1. Tracy Mobley-Martinez, "Word Play," *Gazette* (Colorado Springs, Colo.), 31 January 2010.

2. Ryan McKittrick, "Words from a Zen Garden," *American Repertory Theater*, 1 June 2003.

3. The film version of *Flower Drum Song* in 1961 was the last film to feature an all-Asian American cast until the release of Amy Tan's *The Joy Luck Club* in 1993.

4. Berson, "A Drum with a Difference," 15.

5. Berson, "The Demon," 50.

6. Hwang, "A New Musical."

7. Karen Wada, "A Different Song," *Los Angeles Magazine*, September 2001.

8. Berson, "A Drum with a Difference," 17.

9. Bernard Weinraub, "Fleshing Out Chinatown Stereotypes," *New York Times*, 14 October 2001: Sec 2:7.

10. David Henry Hwang, e-mail message to author, 31 July 2012.

11. Weinraub, "Fleshing Out."

12. Hwang, "A New Musical."

13. Quoted reviews in this paragraph come from the following sources, listed respectively: Ben Brantley, "New Coat of Paint for Old Pagoda," *New York Times*, 18 October 2002: E1; Charles Isherwood, "Repotted *Flower* Lacks Hwang Bang," *Variety*, 21–27 October 2002: 42, 45; and Michael Feingold, "Red, Misread, and Blue," *Village Voice*, 23 October 2002: 64.

14. Quoted reviews in this paragraph come from the following sources, listed respectively: John Lahr, "Despots and Fleshpots," *New Yorker*, 4 November 2002; and Richard Zoglin, "Not Just Chop Suey," *Time*, 28 October 2002.

15. Hwang, *Flower Drum Song*, 12. Subsequent page references appear in the text.

16. Bacalzo, "A Different Drum," 78.

17. Hwang, "A New Musical."

Chapter 7—Wrapping Up, Beginning Anew

1. Hwang, *Trying to Find Chinatown*, in *Trying to Find Chinatown: The Selected Plays*, 287. Subsequent page references appear in the text.

2. Bryer, "David Henry Hwang," 136.

3. Hwang, *Jade Flowerpots and Bound Feet*, 183.

4. Viertel, "Fun with Race," 60.

5. Jeff Lunden, "Hwang's *Yellow Face* to Open in New York," *Morning Edition,* 10 December 2007.

6. Erik Piepenburg, "He Writes about What He Knows," *New York Times,* 2 December 2007.

7. Mary Houlihan, "A Triple Play for Chicago," *Chicago Sun-Times,* 27 June 2011.

8. Paul Hodgins, "Face Time," *Orange County Register* (Santa Ana, Calif.), 19 May 2007.

9. Lunden, "Hwang's *Yellow Face.*"

10. Quoted reviews in this paragraph come from the following sources, listed respectively: Jeremy McCarter, "Holiday Spirit," *New York,* 24–31 December 2007: 102–4; Marilyn Stasio, "*Yellow Face,*" *Variety,* 17–23 December 2007; and Michael Feingold, "This Fun for Hire," *Village Voice,* 19 December 2007: 44.

11. Quoted reviews in this paragraph come from the following sources, listed respectively: Ben Brantley, "A Satirical Spin on Stereotypes, at Home, Abroad and on Broadway," *New York Times,* 11 December 2007; and Frank Scheck, "There's a Bit Too Much *Face* Time," *New York Post,* 11 December 2007.

12. Hwang, *Yellow Face,* 13. Subsequent page references appear in the text.

13. Botelho, "Redefining the Dramatic Canon," 136.

14. Holly Harrison, "Exploring Identity," (Singapore) *Business Times,* 26 April 1996.

15. Hwang, "Stranger Than Fiction," 11.

16. Barbara Chai, "In *Chinglish,* Language Barriers Are a [Bad] Sign of Current Times," *Wall Street Journal,* 10 October 2011: B6.

17. Ken Smith, "*Guanxi* Is Not a Province of China: A Working Definition," *Chinglish* Playbill (July 2011): 13.

18. In the Goodman production Peter was Australian. His character changed nationalities, becoming British for Broadway.

19. Neena Arndt, "A Conversation with Playwright David Henry Hwang," *Goodman Theatre.*

20. Barbara Chai, "Why David Henry Hwang Wrote *Chinglish,*" *Wall Street Journal,* 10 October 2011.

21. Polkow, "Chinglish Lessons."

22. Ibid.

23. The Goodman Theatre held casting calls in Hong Kong, London, Sydney, and Beijing. The play featured Jennifer Lim as Xi, the main female role, and when the play opened on Broadway, she became the first Hong Kong actor to be cast in a lead role on the Great White Way.

24. Jeff Lunden, "*Chinglish* Opens on Broadway," 27 October 2011, National Public Radio, 27 October 2011; transcript.

25. Quoted reviews in this paragraph come from the following sources, listed respectively: Chris Jones, "In Hwang's Hilarious *Chinglish,* the Chinese Tiger Roars, American Business Trembles," *Chicago Tribune,* 27 June 2011; Mary Houlihan, "Impressive Cast in Complex *Chinglish,*" *Chicago Sun-Times,* 27 June 2011; Marilyn Stasio, "*Chinglish,*" *Variety,* 31 October 2011: 51; Ben Brantley, "Can't Talk Very Good Your Language," *New York Times,* 28 October 2011: C1; Hilton Als, "Double Talk," *New Yorker,* 7 November 2011: 86; and Terry Teachout, "The *Follies* of Our Dreams," *Wall Street Journal,* 28 October 2011: D9.

26. Hwang, *Chinglish*, 31. Subsequent page references appear in the text.

27. Charles McNulty, "An Assured Playwright Spans More Comic Barriers," *Los Angeles Times,* 23 October 2011.

28. Hwang, "Stranger Than Fiction," 10.

29. Ibid.

30. Ibid., 11.

BIBLIOGRAPHY

Works by David Henry Hwang

PUBLISHED PLAYS

1000 Airplanes on the Roof: A Science Fiction Music-Drama. Realized with Philip Glass and Jerome Sirlin. Layton, Utah: Gibbs Smith, 1989.

As the Crow Flies. Between Worlds: Contemporary Asian-American Plays. Ed. Misha Berson. New York: TCG, 1990. 97–108.

Chinglish. New York: TCG, 2012.

Flower Drum Song. New York: TCG, 2003.

FOB and Other Plays. New York: Plume, 1990. Comprises *FOB; The Dance and the Railroad; Family Devotions; The House of Sleeping Beauties; The Sound of a Voice; Rich Relations; 1000 Airplanes on the Roof*.

"From Come." *On a Bed of Rice: An Asian-American Erotic Feast*. Ed. Geraldine Kudaka. New York: Anchor, 1995. 456–61.

Golden Child. New York: TCG, 1998.

The Great Helmsman. 2007: The Best Ten-Minute Plays for Three or More Actors. Ed. Lawrence Harbison. Hanover, N.H.: Smith and Kraus, 2008. 31–37.

Jade Flowerpots and Bound Feet. 2004: The Best Ten-Minute Plays for Two Actors. Eds. Michael Bigelow Dixon and Liz Engelman. Hanover, N.H.: Smith and Kraus, 2004. 179–85.

M. Butterfly. New York: Plume, 1989.

Merchandising. Humana Festival '99: The Complete Plays. Lyme, N.H.: Smith and Kraus, 1999. 299–303.

Trying to Find Chinatown: The Selected Plays. New York: TCG, 2000. Comprises *FOB; The Dance and the Railroad; Family Devotions; The Sound of a Voice; The House of Sleeping Beauties; The Voyage; Bondage; Trying to Find Chinatown*.

Yellow Face. New York: TCG, 2009.

ADAPTATIONS

Ibsen, Henrik. *Peer Gynt*. Adapted with Stephan Müller. New York: Playscripts, 2006.

Sis, Peter. *Tibet through the Red Box*. New York: Playscripts, 2006.

FILM AND TELEVISION SCRIPTS

Blind Alleys. Coauthored with Frederic Kimball. Dirs. William Cosel and David F. Wheeler. Metromedia Playhouse, 1985. Television.

The Dance and the Railroad. Dir. Emile Ardolino. ABC Video Enterprises, 1981. Film.

Dances in Exile [Episode for *Alive from Off-Center*]. Dir. Howard Silver. KTCA Minneapolis, 1991. Television.

Forbidden Nights. (Story). Dir. Waris Hussein. Warner Brothers, 1990. Film.

Golden Gate. Dir. John Madden. Samuel Goldwyn, 1994. Film.

Korea: Homes Apart. Dirs. Christine Choy and J. T. Takagi. Third World Newsreel, 1991. Film.

M. Butterfly. Dir. David Cronenberg. Geffen Pictures, 1993. Film.

The Monkey King [also known as *The Lost Empire*]. Dir. Peter MacDonald. Hallmark Entertainment, 2001. Television.

Possession. Coauthored with Neil LaBute and Laura Jones. Dir. Neil Labute. USA Films/Warner Bros., 2002. Film.

UNPUBLISHED WORKS

Aida. Book coauthored with Robert Falls and Linda Woolverton. Music by Elton John and Tim Rice. Dir. Robert Falls. Palace Theatre, New York City, 2000.

Ainadamar. Libretto. Composer Osvaldo Golijov. Tanglewood Musical Center, Lenox, Mass., 2003.

Alice in Wonderland. Libretto with Unsuk Chin. Composer Unsuk Chin. Bavarian State Opera for Munich Opera Festival, 2007.

Bang Kok. Unproduced short-play commission for *Pieces of the Quilt,* San Francisco Magic Theatre, 1995.

Face Value. Colonial Theatre, Boston, 1993.

The Fly. Libretto. Composer Howard Shore. Théâtre du Châtelet, Paris, 2008.

"Hushed Tones." *America: Now and Here* Tour. Kansas City, Mo., March 2011.

Icarus at the Edge of Time. Libretto with Brian Greene. Composer Philip Glass. Alice Tully Hall, New York City, 2010.

"Odysseus on 43rd Street." Lark Play Development Center. April 26, 2012.

The Silver River. Libretto. Composer Bright Sheng. Sante Fe Chamber Music Festival, 1998.

Sound and Beauty. Libretto. Composer Philip Glass. American Repertory Theatre, Cambridge, Mass., 2003.

Tarzan. Book. Music Phil Collins. Richard Rodgers Theatre, New York City, 2006.

Venus Voodoo. Libretto. Composer Lucia Hwong. Lincoln Center, New York City, 1989.

A Very DNA Reunion. The DNA Trail: A Genealogy of Short Plays about Ancestry, Identity, and Confusions. Silk Road Theatre Project, Chicago, 2010.

MISCELLANEOUS PUBLICATIONS

"Afterword." *M. Butterfly.* New York: Plume, 1989. 94–100.

"Are Movies Ready for Real Orientals?" *New York Times* 11 August 1985: 2:1.

"Bringing Up *Child*." *Golden Child.* New York: TCG, 1998. v–ix.

"A Conversation with David Henry Hwang." *Bearing Dream, Shaping Visions: Asian Pacific American Perspectives.* Eds. Linda A. Revilla, Gail M. Nomura, and Shirley Hune. Pullman: Washington State University Press, 1993. 185–89.

"David Henry Hwang." *Between Worlds: Contemporary Asian-American Plays.* Ed. Misha Berson. New York: TCG, 1990. 92–95.

"Evolving a Multicultural Tradition." *MELUS* 16.3 (Fall 1989–90): 16–19.

"Foreword: The Myth of Immutable Culture Identity." *Asian American Drama: 9 Plays from the Multiethnic Landscape.* Ed. Brian Nelson. New York: Applause, 1997. vii–viii.

"Fractures, Large and Small." *American Theatre* December 2009: 62–63.

"In Today's World, Who Represents the 'Real' China?" *New York Times* 1 April 2001: 2:32.

Introduction. *FOB and Other Plays.* New York: Plume, 1990. x–xv.

Introduction. *Flower Drum Song* by C. Y. Lee. New York: Penguin, 2002. xiii–xxi.

Introduction. *Flower Drum Song.* New York: TCG, 2003. ix–xiv.

"Islands in the Mainstream." *The American Theatre Reader.* New York: TCG, 2009. 123–27.

"A New Musical by Rodgers and Hwang." *New York Times* 13 October 2002: 2:1.

"Philip Kan Gotanda." *BOMB* 62 (1998): 20–26.

"People Like Us." *Guardian* 21 April 1989: 21.

"Response." *Yellow Light: The Flowering of Asian American Arts.* Ed. Amy Ling. Philadelphia: Temple University Press, 1999. 222–27.

"Solo." Cowritten with Prince. *Come.* Warner Bros, 1994. Album.

"Stranger Than Fiction." *Newsweek* 23 & 30 April 2012: 10–11.

"Through the Looking Glass: Leading Asian-American Theatre Artists Reflect on the Past Four Decades." *American Theatre* January 2003: 73–85.

"Worlds Apart." *American Theatre* January 2000: 50–56.

Secondary Works

CRITICAL STUDIES, SECTIONS OF BOOKS, MAJOR CRITICAL ARTICLES, AND INTERVIEWS

Bacalzo, Dan. "A Different Drum: David Henry Hwang's Musical 'Revisal' of *Flower Drum Song.*" *Journal of American Drama and Theatre* 15 (Spring 2003): 71–83.

Berson, Misha. "The Demon in David Henry Hwang." *American Theatre,* April 1998: 14–18, 50–51.

———. "A Drum with a Difference." *American Theatre,* February 2002: 14–18, 76.

Botelho, Teresa. "Redefining the Dramatic Canon: Staging Identity Instability in the Work of David Henry Hwang and Chay Yew." *Positioning the New: Chinese American Literature and the Changing Image of the American Literary Canon.* Eds. Tanfer Emin Tunc and Elisabetta Marino. Newcastle upon Tyne: Cambridge Scholars, 2010. 128–42.

Bryer, Jackson R. "David Henry Hwang." *The Playwright's Art: Conversations with Contemporary American Dramatists.* New Brunswick: Rutgers University Press, 1995. 123–46.

Campbell, Karen. "In the Realm of the Voices." *American Theatre,* October 2003: 103–6.

Chang, Williamson B. C. "*M. Butterfly:* Passivity, Deviousness, and the Invisibility of the Asian-American Male." *Bearing Dreams, Shaping Visions: Asian Pacific American Perspectives.* Eds. Linda A. Revilla, Shirley Hune, and Gail M. Nomura. Pullman: Washington State Press, 1993. 181–84.

Cheng, Anne Anlin. "Race and Fantasy in Modern America: Subjective Dissimulation/Racial Assimilation." *Multiculturalism and Representation: Selected Essays.* Eds. John Rieder and Larry E. Smith. Honolulu: University of Hawaii Press, 1996. 175–97.

Cody, Gabrielle. "David Hwang's *M. Butterfly:* Perpetuating the Misogynist Myth." *Theater* 20.2 (1989): 24–27.

Cooperman, Robert. "Across the Boundaries of Cultural Identity: An Interview with David Henry Hwang." *Staging Difference: Cultural Pluralism in American Theatre and Drama.* Ed. Marc Maufort. New York: Peter Lang, 1995. 365–73.

———. "New Theatrical Statements: Asian-Western Mergers in the Early Plays of David Henry Hwang." *Staging Difference: Cultural Pluralism in American Theatre and Drama.* Ed. Marc Maufort. New York: Peter Lang, 1995. 201–13.

Davis, Rocio G. "'Just a Man': Subverting Stereotypes in David Henry Hwang's *M. Butterfly." Hitting Critical Mass* 6.2 (2000): 59–74.

DiGaetani, John Louis. "*M. Butterfly:* An Interview with David Henry Hwang." *Drama Review* 33 (Fall 1989): 141–53.

Dickey, Jerry. "'Myths of the East, Myths of the West': Shattering Racial and Gender Stereotypes in the Plays of David Henry Hwang." *Old West-New West: Centennial Essays.* Ed. Barbara Howard Meldrum. Moscow: University of Idaho Press, 1993. 272–80.

Dong, Lan. "Mulan against Gwan Gung: Performing Myths on a Transnational Stage." *Transnationalism and the Asian American Heroine: Essays on Literature, Film, Myth and Media.* Ed. Lan Dong. Jefferson, N.C.: McFarland, 2010. 103–17.

Eng, David L. "In the Shadows of a Diva: Committing Homosexuality in David Henry Hwang's *M. Butterfly." Asian Sexualities: Dimensions of the Gay and Lesbian Experience.* Ed. Russell Leong. New York: Routledge, 1996. 131–52.

Garber, Marjorie. "The Occidental Tourist: *M. Butterfly* and the Scandal of Transvestism." *Nationalisms and Sexualities.* Eds. Andrew Parker, Mary Russo, Doris Sommer, and Patricia Yaeger. New York: Routledge, 1992. 121–46.

———. *Vested Interests: Cross-Dressing and Cultural Anxiety.* New York: Routledge, 1992.

Grace, Sherrill. "Playing Butterfly with David Henry Hwang and Robert Lepage." *A Vision of the Orient: Texts, Intertexts, and Contexts of* Madame Butterfly. Eds. Jonathan Wisenthal, Sherrill Grace, and Melinda Boyd. Toronto: University of Toronto Press, 2006. 136–51.

Haedicke, Janet V. "David Henry Hwangs's *M. Butterfly:* The Eye on the Wing." *Journal of Dramatic Theory and Criticism* 7:1 (Fall 1992): 27–44.

Jew, Kimberly M. "Dismantling the Realist Character in Velina Hasu Houston's *Tea* and David Henry Hwang's *FOB." Literary Gestures: The Aesthetic in Asian American Writing.* Eds. Rocio G. Davis and Sue-Im Lee. Philadelphia: Temple University Press, 2005. 187–202.

———. "Gothic Aesthetics of Entanglement and Endangerment in David Henry Hwang's *The Sound of a Voice* and *The House of Sleeping Beauties." Asian Gothic: Essays on Literature, Film and Anime.* Ed. Andrew Hock Soon Ng. Jefferson, N.C.: McFarland, 2008. 140–55.

Kerr, Douglas. "David Henry Hwang and the Revenge of Madame Butterfly." *Asian Voices in English.* Eds. Mimi Chan and Roy Harris. Hong Kong: Hong Kong University Press, 1991. 119–30.

Kim, Esther Lee. *A History of Asian American Theatre.* Cambridge: Cambridge University Press, 2006.

Koh, Karlyn. "(Dis)Placing Identities: Cultural Transvestism in David Henry Hwang's *M. Butterfly." West Coast Line* 28.1–2 (1994): 246–54.

Kondo, Dorinne. *About Face: Performing Race in Fashion and Theater*. New York: Routledge, 1997.

Lee, Josephine. *Performing Asian America: Race and Ethnicity on the Contemporary Stage*. Philadelphia: Temple University Press, 1997.

Lee, Quentin. "Between the Oriental and the Transvestite." *Found Object* 8 (Fall 1993): 45–59.

Lin, Hsiu-Chen. "Staging Orientalia: Dangerous 'Authenticity' in David Henry Hwang's *M. Butterfly*." *Journal of American Drama and Theatre* 9.1 (1997): 26–35.

Loo, Chalsa. "*M. Butterfly*: A Feminist Perspective." *Bearing Dreams, Shaping Visions: Asian Pacific American Perspectives*. Eds. Linda A. Revilla, Shirley Hune, and Gail M. Nomura. Pullman: Washington State Press, 1993. 177–80.

Lyons, Bonnie. "'Making His Muscles Work for Himself': An Interview with David Henry Hwang." *Literary Review* 33 (1990): 230–44.

McInturff, Kate. "That Old Familiar Song: The Theatre of Culture in David Henry Hwang's *M. Butterfly*." *A Vision of the Orient: Texts, Intertexts, and Contexts of Madame Butterfly*. Eds. Jonathan Wisenthal, Sherrill Grace, and Melinda Boyd. Toronto: University of Toronto Press, 2006. 72–88.

Moss-Coane, Marty. "David Henry Hwang." *Speaking on Stage: Interviews with Contemporary American Playwrights*. Eds. Philip C. Kolin and Colby H. Kullman. Tuscaloosa: University of Alabama Press, 1996. 277–90.

Moy, James S. "David Henry Hwang's *M. Butterfly* and Philip Kan Gotanda's *Yankee Dawg You Die*: Repositioning Chinese American Marginality on the American Stage." *Theatre Journal* 42.1 (March 1990): 48–56.

———. *Marginal Sights: Staging the Chinese in America*. Iowa City: University of Iowa Press, 1993.

Pao, Angela. "The Critic and the Butterfly: Sociocultural Contexts and the Reception of David Henry Hwang's *M. Butterfly*." *Amerasia Journal* 18.3 (1992): 1–16.

———. "The Eyes of the Storm: Gender, Genre and Cross-Casting in *Miss Saigon*." *Text and Performance Quarterly* 12 (1992): 21–39.

Rabkin, Gerald. "The Sound of a Voice: David Hwang." *Contemporary American Theatre*. Ed. Bruce King. New York: St. Martin's, 1991. 97–114.

Ross, Deborah L. "On the Trail of the Butterfly: David Henry Hwang and Transformation." *Beyond Adaptation: Essays on Radical Transformations of Original Works*. Eds. Phyllis Frus and Christy Williams. Jefferson, N.C.: McFarland, 2010: 111–22.

Rossini, Jon. "From *M. Butterfly* to *Bondage*: David Henry Hwang's Fantasies of Sexuality, Ethnicity, and Gender." *Journal of American Drama and Theatre* 18.3 (2006): 54–76.

Savran, David. "David Hwang." *In Their Own Words: Contemporary American Playwrights*. New York: TCG, 1988. 117–31.

Selim, Yasser Fouad A. "The Theatre of David Henry Hwang: From Hyphenation to the Mainstream." *Positioning the New: Chinese American Literature and the Changing Image of the American Literary Canon*. Eds. Tanfer Emin Tunc and Elisabetta Marino. Newcastle upon Tyne: Cambridge Scholars, 2010. 114–27.

Shimakawa, Karen. "'Who's to Say?' Or, Making Space for Gender and Ethnicity in *M. Butterfly*." *Theatre Journal* 45 (1993): 349–61.

Shin, Andrew. "Projected Bodies in David Henry Hwang's *M. Butterfly* and *Golden Gate*." *MELUS* 27.1 (Spring 2002): 177–96.

Skloot, Robert. "Breaking the Butterfly: The Politics of David Henry Hwang." *Modern Drama* 33.1 (1990): 59–66.

Street, Douglas. *David Henry Hwang*. Boise, Idaho: Boise State University Press, 1989.

Wang, Ban. "Reimagining Political Community: Diaspora, Nation-State, and the Struggle for Recognition." *Modern Drama* 48.2 (2005): 249–71.

Woo, Miseong. "Gender Trouble in Asian American Literature: David Henry Hwang's *The Sound of a Voice*." *Feminist Studies in English Literature* 11.2 (2003): 291–317.

INDEX